BODYPOWER

The secret of self-healing

Vernon Coleman

The classic international bestseller. Chosen by readers of The Good Book Guide as one of the Top 100 books.

NOTE

This book is not intended as an alternative to personal, professional medical advice. The reader should consult a physician in all matters relating to

Reviews of the original edition of *Bodypower*:

`Don't miss it! Dr Coleman's theories could change your life...the revolutionary way to look better and feel younger.' SUNDAY MIRROR

`If you've got *Bodypower* you may never need to visit your doctor again, or take another pill!' SLIMMER

`...a marvellously succinct and simple account of how often the body can heal itself without resort to drugs. It is also refreshingly sensible.' SPECTATOR

`Stimulating, outspoken and easy to understand.' OXFORD MAIL

`Arm yourself with a copy of *Bodypower* - it could make stress a thing of the past.' WOMAN'S WORLD

`This is an excellent book. Very informative and encouraging. Recommended.' NEW HUMANITY

`This is probably one of the most sensible treatises on personal survival that has ever been published...It sets out, in the simplest language, an enormous amount of knowledge about the human mind and body, and it is assimilable in the easiest possible way.' YORKSHIRE EVENING POST

`Despite my own medical training and knowledge of nature's devices, Dr Coleman made me think again...' Book Choice, BBC WORLD SERVICE

`If *Bodypower* really caught on, it could help to save the National Health Service from slow strangulation.' THE SCOTSMAN

`A fascinating read that could change your life.' WHAT DIET

`There are plenty of good books on health care in the shops and for starters I'd recommend *Bodypower* by Dr Vernon Coleman which shows you how to listen to your body and understand its signals.' Angela Willans, WOMANS OWN

`Dr Coleman is one of the most prolific and energetic of literary medical men. He churns out his books with admirable regularity. Every one a gem!' LIVERPOOL ECHO

For a list of other books by Vernon Coleman please see either the Amazon Author page or visit http://www.vernoncoleman.com/

FOREWORD

It began in the autumn of 1980

I was in Vienna and the weather was freezing cold. Outside in the street the wind cut through my thin raincoat as if it wasn't there. I walked with my shoulders hunched and my hands stuffed deep inside my coat pockets. My fingers felt numb. I was so cold that I could hardly think; even my brain felt frozen. I was shivering involuntarily and uncontrollably.

It was dusk. The skies were dark with rain to come and in the early evening gloom the bright lights of the cafe seemed especially warm and promising. I love the cafes of Vienna and Paris. They remind me of the sort of places where Dr Johnson might have talked with friends in London a couple of centuries ago. Through the open curtains I could see the dark wood tables and chairs, the racks of newspapers neatly folded around wooden sticks and the plump,bosomy Austrian waitress hurrying about with vast cups of cream-topped coffee.

I went in, found a table near to the window and sat down. Inside the cafe it was cosy and comfortable. Old-fashioned radiators and a log stove gurgled pleasantly and the air smelt of ground coffee beans and rich chocolate cake. The waitress approached and smiled at me. I gave her my order, took my hands out of my pockets and tried to rub them together. They were white with cold and I could hardly move my fingers.

I cupped my hands, held them up to my face and blew on them. Slowly the feeling came back into them. Slowly the colour returned. Gingerly I flexed and extended my fingers; gradually I regained the movement I had lost.

As I watched my frozen fingers changing colour I suddenly became aware of something that was to change my life. I suddenly became conscious of the remarkable powers of the human body to adapt itself to cope with its environment. Outside in the bitterly cold autumn air the blood had left my fingers to reduce the amount of heat lost in order to try and maintain my internal body temperature. My body had been prepared to sacrifice my fingers to save itself. Inside, in the warmth of the cafe, the blood had rushed back into my hands. Once my body's internal thermometer had recognised that the temperature inside the cafe was warm my body no longer had to fight to keep me alive.

I felt the shivering stop and slipped off my coat. I picked up the coffee which the waitress had brought me and held my head in the steam rising from it.

I'd been qualified as a doctor for ten years and for most of that time I'd been working as a General Practitioner in a small town in central England. To begin with I'd enjoyed the work I did, but for several years I'd been growing more and more worried by the fact that too often I was finding myself interfering with illnesses when it seemed to me that my patients would probably get better by themselves if only I and they were prepared to wait.

Sitting in that cafe in Vienna, with my thawing hands wrapped around a steaming cup of coffee, I realized that the human body has far more extensive, protective and self-healing powers than we give it credit for. I realized that all of us, doctors and patients, tend to be too quick to rush for the medicine cabinet when things go wrong. I remembered a book I'd read when I was at medical school. Called The Wisdom of the Body, it was written in 1932 by a physiologist called W. B. Cannon, who believed that the body's abilities to protect itself from change and threat are comprehensive and far-reaching. And I remembered conversations I'd had with a friend, Tony Sharrock, who was convinced that too often doctors ignore the fact that in illness the body knows best.

I took out my notebook and pencil (for years I have never gone anywhere without both) and immediately wrote down the outline for a book I knew I wanted to write. I called it `Listen to Your Body'. I wanted to try and teach doctors as well as patients that the human body has far-reaching powers that we ignore far too often. I wanted to try and persuade patients to learn to listen to their own bodies and to avoid interfering with their bodies unless absolutely necessary. I wanted to teach doctors that they should not always assume that whenever illness strikes intervention is essential. I wanted to show both patients and doctors that we all underestimate the remarkable healing powers of the human body.

A few days later I got back home full of excitement. I wanted to resign from my practice, write the book and change the world. I knew that I could not remain in General Practice, handing out endless prescriptions. I knew that if I continued to work as a doctor I would not have the time to teach doctors and patients how wrong they were to continue to put all their faith in drugs and surgery.

It wasn't quite that easy.

I sent the outline to my then literary agent with a letter that was bursting with enthusiasm. She was far less impressed than I had hoped she would be. She wrote back to me arguing that `the serious illnesses people have nowadays simply wouldn't heal themselves, so there's a limit to how useful this process can be'. I was frustrated almost beyond belief. That was exactly the attitude I was so desperate to change. The truth is that most illnesses are not serious but are treated as if they are. I insisted that the idea was relevant and valid and that the only way to put forward the idea was to write a book about it, explaining the remarkable self-healing powers of the human body and showing exactly how those powers could be harnessed.

With, I suspect, some reluctance my agent sent the outline out to one or two publishers. They returned it without any enthusiasm. Throughout the early part of 1981 the outline was rejected as irrelevant, impossible or impractical by half the publishers in London.

But the book had already changed my life irrevocably. In the summer of 1981 I resigned from the National Health Service and decided to become a full-time professional writer. The more time I spent researching material for the book I now called *Bodypower* the more convinced I was that I could not justify the work I was doing as a GP. As a practising doctor I just did not have the time to explain to my patients why I didn't always want to give them prescriptions. I needed to stand outside everyday practice in order to spread the philosophy that seemed to me to be so important.

Leaving the NHS wasn't the wrench I'd thought it might be. I missed my patients desperately but I didn't miss the NHS bureaucrats. My last few months of existence as a GP were a constant battle.

It wasn't until 1982 that I found a publisher prepared to commission the book. I was having dinner with Jamie Camplin of Thames and Hudson to celebrate the launch of my book The Good Medicine Guide when I managed to persuade him that the principles behind *Bodypower* were not only sound but that they also merited a wider audience. Camplin agreed to publish the book.

The dream I'd had in that cafe in Vienna two and a half years earlier had been fulfilled. The philosophy I described in *Bodypower* changed my life, and has influenced everything I've written about medicine since 1980. It has also influenced hundreds of medical writers, thousands of doctors and millions of patients. The *Bodypower* philosophy is now widely acknowledged and accepted.

Every week since 1983 I have collected new evidence showing the remarkable powers of the human body. There has been evidence from scientists around the world showing that the power of the body and the mind is greater than anyone could have dreamt a mere decade ago. For example, researchers have shown that crying helps the body get rid of harmful waste material. It has been shown that tears shed because of emotional feelings contain more protein than tears shed because of irritation. When you are upset and you cry your body is getting rid of unwanted and dangerous wastes. Researchers have also shown that during the last three months of pregnancy, and for the twelve months after a pregnancy has ended, a mother's lips produce sexually attractive chemicals designed to make her lips more kissable. Sebaceous glands along the borders of the newborn baby's lips produce similar chemicals and help ensure that the baby responds to its mother's kisses in an appropriate way.

Newspaper stories have supported the *Bodypower* theory too. Soon after *Bodypower* was published I read about a farm worker who had been involved in a horrific accident. He carried his severed arm for a mile in order to get help. His arm was then sewn back on by a surgeon at a nearby hospital. More recently I read of an 87 year old widow who knotted sheets together and climbed out of her first floor window in order to escape from a fire. In both these cases the human body found resources that no one would have thought could exist.

Most exciting of all, perhaps, has been the response from the medical profession. When *Bodypower* was first published the response from some parts of the medical establishment was cool. Doctors have for decades been taught that in order to beat disease they have to interfere with nature. The medical profession has grown in strength alongside the drugs industry; thousands of doctors have been taught that a doctor's first response to any illness must always be to reach for his prescription pad. But that too has changed. More and more often the medical journals now contain articles written by doctors explaining how they have discovered that it isn't always necessary to interfere when a patient falls ill; that the body can often look after itself; that the body's defence mechanisms and self-healing mechanisms are far more sophisticated than they had been taught and that the power of the human mind is far greater than anyone would have dared suggest just ten years ago.

In 1983 the philosophy behind *Bodypower* seemed new and slightly frightening to many people. Some thought it threatening, a few even suggested that it was heresy to suggest that in 90 per cent of all illnesses there was no need for a professional healer, that the body could look after itself perfectly well.

Today the philosophy described in *Bodypower* is widely accepted. It has not halted the march of modern interventionism but it has, perhaps, caused some of those who lead the march to break step. From the letters I have received I know that it has encouraged many to be prepared to take advantage of their bodies' own healing processes and to regard illness as something to be conquered in partnership with the help of healers (whether orthodox or alternative) rather than as something to be handed over completely to the professionals.

If this is the first time you've read *Bodypower* I hope you find it as exhilarating as I still do. I hope it changes your life too!

Vernon Coleman Devon, England

PREFACE

Bodypower is above all a practical book. The aim is to help you use your body's own inbuilt powers in order to deal safely and effectively with the many, varied hazards which are an inevitable part of modern life.

The book is divided into four parts. In Part One I have described many of the body's remarkable mechanisms and explained

how those mechanisms operate.

In Part Two I have produced an account of the ways in which most of us normally attempt to deal with signs and symptoms of disease. I have explained why I think that the traditional `interventionist' approach is often inappropriate.

In many ways these first two parts are `introductory' sections. They are, nevertheless, essential in providing the background for the more important practical guidance that follows.

In Part Three I have outlined the fundamental principles of the*Bodypower*philosophy. And in Part Four I have described some of the practical ways in which it can be sued to advantage. *Bodypower*can be used to help provide you with protection against disease, to help speed recovery, to help improve your physical and mental capacities in the face of the many different threats to health.

Bodypower is not a gimmick. and it does not consist of any trickery. *Bodypower* is a new approach to life based on sound, physiological principles.

Vernon Coleman

PART 1: THE WORLD WITHIN

Our bodies are sensitive, delicate and remarkably frail. The fact that we manage to prosper in a world which is often hostile and unsympathetic to our needs is a tribute to a vast number of automatic mechanisms - mechanisms specifically designed to enable us to survive an infinite variety of environmental hazards, to repair and restore ourselves to good health when disease and disability threaten and to learn from our experiences so that we can improve our capacity to survive.

Many of these mechanisms are complex, sophisticated and difficult to understand. It is perhaps because of this that we usually see the human body in terms of the mechanical world with which we are familiar. So, some centuries ago, when physiologists were first struggling to explain precisely how the brain manages to send messages around the body and exactly how the heart succeeds in keeping blood flowing through the vessels, it was perhaps natural that they should choose to offer their explanations in mechanical terms, using as analogies the only physical concepts they understood.

In the seventeenth century, for example, Rene Descartes argued that the nerves which connect our brains to our muscles are filled with fluid and work on a simple hydraulic system. That theory was accepted for many years but then, when Alexander Graham Bell gave us the telephone and the telephone companies gave us switchboards, it became fashionable to describe the central nervous system as some extraordinarily complicated network of telephone lines connecting thousands of separate callers with one another. More recently, when computers became commonplace and it was found that some nerve endings had electrical connections, indicating that nerve messages may sometimes be transmitted with the aid of electrical impulses, it became common to compare the human brain to the computer.

This recurrent tendency to see the human body in simplistic terms and to explain the mechanisms which exist in terms of devices which we ourselves have created has the dangerous and restricting effect of ensuring that the observer must inevitably fail to comprehend the full range of human capabilities. Indeed, it seems that too many modern scientists deny or ignore new evidence because it does not fit in with what they want to believe, or because it suggests that the manmade systems which are regarded with such awe and respect are by no means as sophisticated or as advanced as they might like to think them to be.

Today we are only beginning to understand the extent of our ignorance about the human body. Slowly it is becoming clear that if a scientist claims that there is a simple explanation for a complex phenomenon, then he is probably wrong. Our knowledge about the human body is expanding so quickly that it is almost certainly true to say that anything a student learns about the physiology of the human body will be out of date by the time he leaves his school, college or university.

We now find that the traditional dividing line between the conscious and the unconscious mind can no longer be drawn with any accuracy. We know today that messages are transmitted within the brain by five different types of electrical activity and by a complex network of chemical messengers which are far more bewildering than our predecessors ever imagined.

We know that the brain contains pain-relieving hormones and, although we do not understand why, we know that it can be affected by magnetic storms. We understand some of the driving forces which control our lives but, although the desire to enjoy sex and the desire to win may be forces which we can explain, we still do not know enough about the mind to be able to define such intangible concepts as pleasure, jealousy or love. We may be able to explain why a man should find a woman attractive but how do we obtain pleasure from the sight of a beautiful sunset or an exquisite painting? What physiological purpose or evolutional value can there be in such abstract pleasures?

Amidst all the confusion and ignorance, the one thing that we can say with certainty is that the capacity of the human body to heal itself, to benefit from experience, to improve itself, to protect itself and to guard itself against threats of all kinds is far greater than we have ever imagined it to be.

On the pages which follow you'll find descriptions of some of the many physiological properties and mechanisms which have been reported. Many of these mechanisms pose questions which we cannot begin to answer and the existence of some of them must result in the serious questioning of established theories about how the body works. My aim is to show the extraordinary capacity of the human body to look after itself, and to provide a scientific background for the later sections of this book, in which I shall describe how and why an understanding of your body can help you look after yourself more effectively. My intention is to show the extent of only some of the body's resources - resources which are often unsuspected and frequently unused, resources which we do not thoroughly understand but which are nevertheless of inestimable value.

Your body has internal mechanisms which regulate the way you act and react

Anyone for tennis?

If you reach out your hand to pick up a pencil your brain will control all the necessary muscles by using your body's inbuilt information-collecting system. If your hand looks like overshooting the pencil, appropriate messages will be sent to your brain. And the muscles which are promoting that particular movement will quickly go into reverse. If your hand is aiming to the left of the pencil, the muscles which are taking your hand that way will be relaxed and the muscles which will move your hand to the right will be contracted. Your brain is using what the engineers call `feedback mechanisms' to enable it to control your hand with precision and to ensure that it is successful in picking up the pencil. Small sensory cells deep inside the muscles provide the brain with vital information about the positions of individual muscles and the position of the whole arm, which is matched with the information provided by the eyes.

Picking up a pencil is a fairly trivial task, of course. If you are playing tennis, thousands and thousands of feedback mechanisms have to be brought into play. Your brain has to judge the speed and curve of the ball and must use information from a vast number of sensory cells in order to ensure that the right muscles contract at the right moment and for precisely the correct length of time. Your feet have to be in the right place and your hand has to move in the right way. All these movements have to be carried out very quickly and, if you have played tennis before, your body will have acquired muscle experiences which will enable it to make them that much quicker. In effect, your muscles will have been programmed to enable you to play tennis.

Guided missiles, equipped both with propulsion systems and sensory systems, do very much the same sort of thing in a much cruder way. Your body has a number of advantages and subtleties that the most sophisticated manmade guidance systems do not have. You, for example, can produce an infinite variety of different shots, and you can use your experiences to create new solutions to old problems. You can even repair yourself if you fall and graze an arm or sprain an ankle.

But there are even more important differences: however skilful technicians may be when they are preparing guidance systems they cannot ensure that their missiles are programmed with a burning will to succeed. Nor can they add any extra circuits to make sure that a computer-controlled missile system enjoys its work or gains pleasure from winning. When you are playing tennis you can be driven and motivated by an almost unending series of driving forces that cannot be explained in purely mechanical terms. What does a machine know about anger, jealousy, resentment, pride, indignation, humour, love, conscience or guilt? What can it know of the hundred and one other preferences, values and feelings which together enable us to balance facts against ambitions, experiences and aspirations and come up with decisions which may be irrational and inexplicable but none the less right?

The choice is yours

Your brain contains about 1000 billion cells. Each one of those cells has something like 5,000 connections with neighbouring cells. And every minute of every hour of every day those cells and those connections are buzzing with information. Message carrying impulses are continually reaching your brain from your sensory cells, from the special receptors in your muscles which carry information about limb positions, from the chemically sensitive receptors in your blood vessels which continually provide up-dated information about the levels of various constituents in your blood, from your special sense organs - and from a thousand and one other independent sources. The information never stops coming. Even when you are asleep there is still a very heavy traffic of news coming into your brain.

Theoretically, all this data is significant. Abd yet since it would obviously be impossible from your brain to respond to every single piece of information it receives, many of the impulses must be ignored. A small amount of the information that gets through will eventually produce a voluntary response; some of it will produce an automatic response from one of the many mechanisms which ensure that the internal environment is maintained in tiptop condition. But most will be ignored. If it were not, your brain would be continually confused by an unending series of conflicting reports and opposing instructions. Your brain's inbuilt ability to select the information that needs action is therefore of vital importance.

In order to ensure that the right information is ignored and that the right information produces a response, the human brain has developed a delightfully simple way of solving what could be a difficult problem. At the same time, it has managed to solve this potential problem in such a way that it can also keep all sensory receptors tuned to respond to very slight changes. Those sensory receptors are, in fact, adjusted to such a delicate level that every minute thousands will fire off false alarms.

Your brain deals with this deluge of information by looking for patterns among the news messages it is getting and by responding only when something like a hundred more or less identical impulses are received. This very simple arrangement ensures that your billions of brain cells are able to pick the relevant from the irrelevant with considerable ease. Isolated bits of unsubstantiated news are ignored. News trends produce action.

The unconscious mind

It is sometimes thought that there is a firm dividing line between what goes on in the conscious mind and what goes on in the unconscious mind. In practice, however, there seems to be no division at all. There is plentiful evidence to suggest that our unconscious minds are, indeed, capable of responding to external stimuli as well as our conscious minds. We can, it seems, switch ourselves onto automatic pilot with amazing ease.

There is, for example, evidence that epileptics have successfully ridden bicycles while they were technically not conscious. There is a well-authenticated anecdote which describes how an epileptic doctor managed to see a clinic full of patients without being in the slightest bit aware of what was going on. You yourself have probably experienced something similar if you drive a car. Most drivers have at one time or another `woken up' with a start to find that they have been driving the car quite safely without being in any way aware of their actions. Operating the controls according to the instructions of the unconscious mind means that the requirements of the conscious mind are ignored - I once set off to drive from London to Coventry and found myself on the outskirts of Bristol without much idea of how I got there.

Sometimes this unconscious awareness can be extremely useful. When windmills were used for grinding flour it was well known that the millers would be woken up if the mill stopped turning and needed attention. The rumbling of the stones and the rush of the wind in the sails didn't stop the millers sleeping - the absence of those noises did.

I had a similar experience during a recent bad winter when I woke in the middle of the night with a jump. I sat upright in bed, convinced that I must have been woken by the sound of a burglar. In fact, like the millers, I'd been woken not by a noise but by an absence of noise. Because the weather was so bad, I'd decided to leave the central heating switched on for the night in order to ensure that the pipes didn't freeze. The boiler makes a noise as it pumps hot water round the house and when the noise had suddenly stopped I had been woken by the silence. My sleeping mind had immediately recognised that the absence of that particular noise might be a threat and I'd woken up before the house had had time to start going cold.

Central eating control

Hidden deep inside your brain there is an impressive device known as an appetite control centre. The power of this unique control centre is astonishing. It can make sure that you never get overweight or underweight. And it can make sure that you never become short of essential vitamins or minerals.

The importance and remarkably wide-reaching authority of this part of the brain was identified in research done by Dr Clara M Davis of Chicago in the 1920s. Writing in the American Journal of Diseases of Children in October 1928 she described experiments she'd done with newly weaned infants.

Her aim was to find out whether these young children could:

1 Choose their own food and eat enough to stay alive.

2 Select a good balance of meat and vegetables

3 Pick foods designed to keep them healthy.

The results were staggering. Dr Davis found that without any prompting the infants chose good, varied diets. Their growth rates, development, vigour and appearance were just as satisfactory as those of babies who had been eating foods carefully chosen by experts. They ate the right types of food and they ate the correct quantities. And they stayed perfectly healthy.

Five years later, in a paper read at the 75th Annual Session of the American Dental Association, in conjunction with the Chicago Centennial Dental Congress, Dr Davis gave details of more research that she had done.

Having studied 15 infants for between 6 months and 4 1/2 years she had come to the conclusion that all were able to select a good variety of satisfying foods and to ensure that they ate neither too much nor too little. Despite the fact that hardly any of the children had had more than a taste of spinach or cabbage they all remained healthy. Their eating habits seemed to be unplanned, even chaotic, but none ever had stomach ache or became constipated. The only bouts of diarrhoea that occurred were the result of infections. None of the children who were allowed to choose their own food became chubby or fat.

Some years later, during the Second World War, research showed that when soldiers were allowed access to unlimited supplies of food the troops ate just what their bodies needed according to their environment. Without any professional prompting, they automatically chose a mixture of protein, fat and carbohydrate that nutrition experts would describe as ideal.

Listen to your body when it tells you what - and how much - you need to eat and you'll stay slim and well fed for life. There would be no need for dieting books, professional nutritionists or slimming clubs if we'd only learn to let our appetite control centres take over.

Breast is best

The female breasts were originally designed for use as feeding aids rather than devices to titillate the male of the species. They are particularly well designed for their purpose. Milk production begins at the right moment and will usually continue for as long as it is needed. And as far as the baby is concerned, mother's milk really is best. Not only does is contain a perfect balance of essential constituents, but it also gives the baby a useful mixture of mother's antibodies which will provide the consumer with temporary protection against a wide range of diseases.

There is another advantage too. Some years ago doctors noticed that breastfed children are much less likely to get fat than bottle fed children. It was found that the contents of breast milk change when the baby has had enough to drink and that this change in the constituents triggers off the end of the baby's feeding response.

The rhythm and the blues

The spinning of the earth round its central axis structures our lives. It is this spinning which gives us our days and our nights and which provides us with a pattern for living. We sleep and work, rest and play, eat and drink according to the daily rhythm which results from the earth's movement.

Nevertheless, important as this daily rhythm is, there are known to be many other physiological, psychological and biomedical rhythms which also have an effect on the way we live. Of these, the best known is the one which ensures that a woman's hormone levels will rise and fall in such a way that she will alternately ovulate and menstruate, allowing each fresh egg to have its day, then seeing that it is discarded before fresh pastures are prepared in the womb. Surprisingly, we know little or nothing about this twenty-eight day clock inside each woman which is capable of operating relatively smoothly for some twenty or thirty years.

There are other body rhythms about which we know no more. There is, for example, an internal clock which controls body temperature from day to day. The fact that this clock seems to match the clock which regulates the menstrual cycle means that women can judge the best time to conceive by taking their temperature each day. Yet we know little or nothing about the clock mechanism involved.

Nor do we know why more people die at 4.00 a.m. than at any other time of day. Or why suicide is more common in the spring and the autumn when duodenal ulcers are also especially likely to perforate. Or why the best time to learn anything is just before you go to sleep. Or why the best time for making important decisions is round the middle of the day. Or why most men are sexually at their best early in the morning. Or why most of us are most alert during the early evening.

What we do know is that there seems to be a relationship between body rhythms and health. There is evidence, for example, that there is a link between depression and some sort of body rhythm. In an article published in the British Medical Journal in 1976, Nikitopoulou and Crammer showed that there is a change in the daily temperature rhythm in patients suffering from a particular type of depression. Other researchers have found the same thing. But as yet no one seems to know whether these patients are depressed because their body clocks are disordered or whether their body clocks are disordered because they are depressed. However, there is one clue which suggests that it is when the body rhythm goes wrong that depression strikes. It seems that a drug called lithium can be used to help some depressed patients. And when it works, lithium seems to slow the body rhythm down to normal. There may, therefore, be a link between lithium, a body clock and the mental state of an individual.

There is another clue too. Back in 1938 G.M. Griffiths and J.T. Fox published a paper in The Lancet in which they reviewed 110 male epileptics who lived in an English city called Lichfield. The men had a total of 39,920 fits during the period in which they were under observation. By making a careful note of the time of day when these fits occurred, Griffiths and Fox discovered that many of the epileptics had their fits at a regular time of day. It may well be, therefore, that epilepsy can sometimes be a result of a disordered body clock.

We know also that there are several different clocks which govern what takes place when we are asleep. These produce massive changes in hormone levels, a fall in the body temperature and a change in the rate of body hair growth. Electroencephalographic recordings taken in special sleep laboratories have even shown that there are two different types of sleep which alternate throughout the night. Rapid Eye Movement sleep is characterised by the fact that the muscles of the head and neck become floppy, the eyes jerk and the tone of the muscles round the rest of the body varies a good deal. Men often develop erections during REM sleep and dreams are frequently very active. Non Rapid Eye Movement sleep, on the other hand, is characterised by the absence of eye movements, a lowering of the pulse rate and blood pressure and a generalised lowering of muscle tone.

We understand little enough about these changes. We know no more about many others. Why, for example, should the amount of iron in the blood be greater in the morning than in the evening? Why should the amount of serum zinc in the blood fall in the morning? Why should the frequency of sexual intercourse be considerably greater during the months of April to June than during the latter part of the year? And how do we explain the fact that a study done in the Netherlands showed that people born in the winter months had a greater chance of eventually developing carcinoma of the bronchus than those born during the summer?

There are, of course, many individuals who strongly believe that these rhythms govern all aspects of human life. For some years now some people have believed that their health and fortune is ordained not by the position of the stars but by three different body cycles. In a book called The Periods of Human Life, published in 1904, Hermann Swoboda, Professor of Psychology at Vienna University, announced that our physical vitality and strength is governed by a 23-day cycle and that our emotional strength and stability is governed by a 28-day cycle. A few years later, Professor Alfred Teltscher of Innsbruck declared that there is a third, 33-day cycle, which governs intellectual activity.

All three of these cycles are said to begin on the individual's birthday and to follow a wave pattern after that, with the waves repeating themselves after 23,28 and 33 days. The theory is that the peaks and troughs of the cycle are the most critical times and that on these days an individual is particularly likely to be at his best or his worst.

By a careful study of the way the three waves relate to one another it is said to be possible to select the most suitable time of the month for particular types of action. It is alleged, for example, that if the date of a surgical operation is picked with care then the patient's recovery will be speedy and smooth. One published survey decided that over 30 per cent of all deaths from surgical misadventure could be prevented by avoiding dates when the patients' biorhythms were unfavourable.

The information we have is tantalising. Some body clocks seem to be controlled by hormones released by the pituitary gland or the hypothalamus. Others seem to be controlled without the use of any circulating hormones. There seem to be some clocks which can be controlled voluntarily, for there are individuals who claim that they can make themselves wake up simply by switching on an internal alarm clock.

However many separate clocks there are, however they may be controlled and whatever their role may be, there is no denying the fact each one of us has inside us a complex series of timing mechanisms which have a powerful effect on the way we tick.

The sex drive

Doctors treating Parkinson's Disease have on many occasions reported that their patients have been sexually stimulated by a drug called L Dopa, which is commonly used to help control the symptoms of the disease. In several surveys nearly all the patients reported that while taking the drug they noticed an increase in their sexual interest. One eighty-year-old man began having erotic dreams and nocturnal emissions. Another man, aged seventy-six, became so lustful that his nurses complained about his behaviour. A female patient given the drug tore off all her clothes and tried to seduce the male patients and staff. A thirty-seven-year-old patient had unexpected and embarrassing erections when he was playing ping pong with a nurse.

The reason for this unexpected sexual activity seems to be that L Dopa has an effect on the levels of dopamine and serotonin, two chemicals which occur naturally in the brain. Puzzled researchers have shown that dopamine increases sexual activity while serotonin inhibits it; the balance between the two chemicals controls an individual's sexual activities.

Although we still don't know precisely how it works, it seems that the body has an inbuilt mechanism designed to ensure that the survival of the species is not threatened by any lack of sexual desire.

There are mechanisms which enable you to adapt to changing demands

Adaptability

In 1936 the Hungarian pistol-shooting champion represented his country in the Olympic Games as a right-handed shot. In 1939, having lost his right arm in an accident in 1938, he became World Champion as a left-handed marksman.

That individual achievement is just one rather dramatic example of the many ways in which the human body can reallocate resources and skills and adapt itself for survival and success. Something similar, although obviously less spectacular, happens almost every day to each one of us. If you go into a room in which there is no light and you cannot see, your other senses will become much sharper than usual. You may stumble a bit, but you'll be able to find your way around by using your hearing, your sense of touch and your sense of smell. The loss of one sense automatically encourages your brain to make extra use of your other senses.

This simple process of adaptation is even more noticeable among individuals who are permanently blind and deaf. The blind, for example,can often manage to make progress in an unfamiliar environment with relatively little blundering. Hearing, smell and touch will be replacing the missing vital images.

This ability to adapt to new circumstances is perhaps one of the most remarkable human skills. It explains why people with paralysed legs often develop strong arms and why individuals who are so crippled that they can hardly walk can often swim well. You can prove to yourself just how adaptable your body is by walking round the house with a slipper on one foot and a heavy boot on the other. You'll soon find that your body adapts to the different weights. Indeed, if you take off the heavy boot and replace it with the other slipper, you'll find that to begin with you have some difficulty in walking. Your body will have adapted so well that you will be temporarily overcompensating for the weight of the non-existent boot.

Incidentally, if you have ever been impressed by stories of American Indian trackers who are able to follow prey for miles by using their senses, you may be interested to hear that in some modern prisons, where the law of the jungle tends to operate with a vengeance, prisoners are reported to have acquired considerable hunting skills. One prisoner, for example, has claimed that he can identify individual warders by their breathing patterns, their scent and the creaking of their arthritic joints. He's also shown that he can smell a packet of cigarettes in a coat pocket several yards away.

Your variable pump

Without a good, steady flow of blood no part of your body can do its job properly. Blood carries oxygen and food supplies and also removes the waste products. Neither your brain nor your kidneys, your liver nor your lungs, can work effectively or efficiently without an adequate supply of fresh blood. Even your heart, the powerful muscular pump which is responsible for ensuring that between 10 and 50 pints of blood are sent through your arteries every minute of every day of your life, needs a supply of its own.

Naturally the precise amounts of blood that the various parts of your body need will vary from minute to minute according to the work that has to be done. If you are sitting in a chair reading a book, your muscles are not going to need very much oxygen or food. The blood will be able to wander round at a relatively gentle pace. On the other hand, if you are racing for a bus or running away from a couple of muggers, your muscles will need a considerable amount of oxygen and food in order to cope with the sudden extra workload.

A number of very delicately balanced mechanisms exist to ensure that the amount of blood circulating matches your body's requirements. If some sudden emergency means that you have to leap out of your chair, your heart will not only beat faster, it will also increase its output every time it beats. This will mean that the amount of blood (and therefore the amount of oxygen and food) that will reach your muscles will be automatically increased.

Feeling on top of the world

When mountain climbers have taken on the world's highest peaks they have invariably allowed themselves time to acclimatise. When the Olympic Games were held in Mexico City some years ago many athletes arrived in Mexico months before the games were due to start.

Neither climbers nor athletes worried about getting used to the food. Their concern was to make sure they allowed their bodies time to get used to te low level of oxygen that is present in the atmosphere at high altitudes. The Himalayas and Mexico City have one important thing in common: both are many thousands of feet above sea level.

Since the efficiency of a human body depends very much on oxygen, living and working at high altitudes may appear to pose tremendous problems. The red blood cells which normally pick up oxygen in the lungs and then carry it round the rest of the body cannot collect enough oxygen from the air to which they have access. And that can mean that the whole organism performs poorly.

This only happens, however, to people who have recently moved into high altitude areas. Anyone who spends a month or two at a high altitude will slowly begin to adapt to lower levels of oxygen. The most important part of that adaptation is the formation of many new red blood cells. Faced with thinner air and less oxygen, the human body simply increases the number of red blood cells which are available to carry oxygen round in the blood. A healthy male who can manage very well with a mere 5,000,000 red blood cells per cubic millimetre of blood at sea level will have up to 8,000,000 red blood cells per cubic millimetre of blood when he has spent a little time living at 12,000 feet.

What a nerve!

The human nervous system is often compared to the computer. The analogy is false in many respects, but it perhaps looks weakest when you consider the ways in which the nervous system can repair itself when it is damaged. When a patient has a stroke he may be temporarily paralysed down one side of his body and may completely lose the ability to speak. Within months, however, the paralysis may disappear and the ability to speak may return. Damage that may have looked horrifyingly permanent often turns out not to be.

These self-healing improvements take place because the many individual cells which make up the nervous system are not only capable of making new connections and of rebuilding shattered circuits but can even vary their responses according to special demands and local conditions. Some nerve cells can regenerate and grow back into position when they have been cut, crushed or damaged. And when nerves are beyond self-repair, neighbouring cells can sometimes take over the contacts that would otherwise have been lost. You can lose quite large chunks of your brain without ever noticing that anything has happened.

Scientists still do not understand how all this happens. Some say that chemicals are released in order to attract new fibres along appropriate pathways. Others argue that electrical gradients control the nerve cell movements. And a third group of scientists believe that the path of a regenerating nerve cell may be guided by some unseen mechanical map.

The explanation may still be a mystery. The facts, however, are undeniable.

Pink, brown and black

When white or pink skin is exposed to the sun a number of things happen. The most dramatic consequence is that cells deep inside the skin start to release a substance called melanin which slowly migrates towards the surface. Melanin is the pigment which turns the skin brown. Its purpose is to provide some protection against further damage.

Dark-skinned people, originating from the hotter countries of the world, are born with a protective layer of melanin on the outer skin surface.: the hotter the county, the blacker the skin.

Thus it is just possible that - since they are now sharing an identical climate - eventually all the inhabitants of South Africa will have skin of exactly the same colour. By the same token those people of African origin who now live in Northern, temperate climates could have white descendants in a few hundred thousand years. They no longer need melanin-enriched skin.

Muscle bound

If you do a lot of heavy lifting you'll develop muscles in all the right places. Those Mr Universe types who acquire muscles on their muscles on their muscles have merely taken advantage of the body's ability to build additional muscle tissue wherever it seems to be needed. If you need particular muscles to be well developed in order to do your job properly, those muscles will slowly develop as you do the job. Your body can build itself and shape itself to suit your requirements. And if the requirements change, so can your body's distribution of muscle tissue.

Them bones, them bones

If you fall down and fracture a bone your body will be perfectly capable of repairing the damage so effectively that you will soon be able to forget that the fracture ever took place. If two parts of the broken bone have been moved a long way from one another, outside help may be needed to re-position the bone fragments in such a way that healing can take place. In the majority of cases, however, that is the only outside interference that is needed. The body's ability to repair itself will deal with the rest of the problem.

An elaborate system of hormone controls will ensure that the mended bone is neither too thick nor too frail, that it has the proper shape and that it is organised internally so as to be capable of withstanding the most severe types of stress.

Most amazing, perhaps is the fact that the decisions which will govern the way that the bone is rebuilt are not simply made according to some arbitrary, unbendable rules, but can be altered according to both environmental influences at the injury site and information which has been picked up as a result of previous experiences of a similar nature.

Break a bone and your body will repair the damage to make the new bone stronger than the bone you broke.

Feet made for walking

Should you use your hands a great deal to perform heavy manual work you'll eventually develop callosities on the skin. These thickened, rather unsightly patches of coarse, hard, yellowish skin develop in response to unusual amounts of pressure. The cells in the horny layer of the skin proliferate so as to make the skin tougher just where it needs to be toughest.

The same sort of thing can happen on other parts of your body. If you do a lot of walking you'll develop callosities on your feet. These thickened patches of skin may not look very attractive, but they do ensure that the skin is hard wearing in places where it needs to be hard wearing. Wouldn't it be useful if shoes could automatically strengthen themselves in the places where they usually wear out?

The housemaid's knee and the student's elbow

If you do a lot of kneeling on hard surfaces you'll acquire a soft, squashy swelling over your knee cap. You'll have what is known technically as a `pre-patella bursitis' but popularly as housemaid's knee. A slightly different type of swelling, which occurs when the kneeling is done in a rather more upright position, is known as `tibial tubercule bursitis', or parson's knee.

If you spend your time sitting with your head held in your hands and your elbow pressed hard on your desk you'll acquire a soft squashy swelling over your elbow. That's known as an `olecranon bursitis', or student's elbow.

Bursae ca, in fact, develop wherever the skin is stretched tight across a prominent bone and then subjected to pressure. The fluid that fills a bursa is deliberately put there by your body in order to provide a natural cushion. You may find the swelling rather unsightly and it may be uncomfortable. But it does protect the skin and the bone from more serious damage.

Old blue eyes

Have you ever stopped to ask yourself why some people should have blue eyes while others have brown eyes? Even if you have found the question worth considering, I expect you have concluded that the answer is not much more than a simple quirk of nature. Some people just happen to have irises which are coloured blue. Others have irises that are coloured brown.

Naturally, however, things are not as simple as that. In 1975 Michel Millodot of the Department of Ophthalmic Optics at the University of Wales Institute of Science and Technology published a paper in Nature showing that blue-eyed people have more sensitive corneas than brown-eyed people. He showed that there is a steady grading between people who have bright blue eyes and whose eyes are very sensitive, and people who have dark brown eyes and whose eyes are much less sensitive to the light. Similarly, individuals with hazel eyes are slightly less sensitive than those with blue eyes, while those with green eyes are less sensitive than those with hazel eyes. If your eyes are dark brown, they'll be less sensitive than the lighter brown eyes of someone else.

The clue to the explanation of all this lies in the fact that dark-skinned people who originated from the sunnier parts of the world invariably have dark brown eyes. Light blue eyes, on the other hand, are commonest among people born and bred in Northern Europe, where the sun is a less frequent visitor.

Since eyes which are dark brown are only one quarter as sensitive as eyes which are bright blue, it is clear that blacks are effectively born with built-in shades.

The eyes have it

In 1928 experiments started by Theodore Erismann at the University of Innsbruck set out to show how adaptable the human eyes can be.

To begin with, Erismann's subjects were given special goggles, which put a prism directly in front of each eye, but in addition the Austrian worked with goggles which transposed the visual field from top to bottom or from left to right. He even had a pair of spectacles which enabled the wearer to see only to the rear - as though he had eyes in the back of his head.

The subjects who bravely wore these extraordinary goggles found that within a week or two their eyes adapted very well. For example, after several weeks of wearing goggles that transposed left and right, one of the subjects working with Erismann found that he had adapted so successfully that he was able to drive his motorcycle through Innsbruck while still wearing them.

More recently, Ivo Kohler of the University of Innsbruck has described what happened when he designed special goggles which created a blue-tinted world as the wearer looked to the left and a yellow-tinted world as he looked to the right. Kohler found that his subjects even managed to adapt to these spectacles and that the colour distortions disappeared. Somehow the eyes and the visual system as a whole managed to introduce a corrective factor which ensured that the confusing effect of the goggles was overcome.

Kohler has also managed to show that the eyes can adapt to variable as well as constant distortions. Consider, for example, an experiment he did with a pair of spectacles in which the lenses had been fitted with prisms which had their bases pointing to the right. At the start of the experiment with these spectacles the subject found that if he turned his head to the left and then glanced to the right he would see an image that steadily contracted. Conversely, if he turned his head to the right and then glanced to the left he would see an expanding image. The prism had distorted his whole sense of vision.

After no more than a few weeks, this distortion disappeared and the eyes somehow managed to adapt to their new world, learning to expand contracting images and to contract expanding images according to the position of the head and the eyes. When, after wearing the spectacles for this period, the subject removed them, he found that the adaptation continued to operate. The result was that he found himself seeing a world which was a mirror image of the world he had first seen when he had put on the special prism spectacles. This effect slowly disappeared over a few more days as the eyes learned that the adaptation processes they had developed were no longer necessary.

Such research may seem bizarre, but it does show very clearly that the eyes are not rigid structures capable only of passing image to the brain like twin film cameras. On the contrary, they are extremely adaptable and sensitive organs which can change their mode of adaptation to cope with almost any demands.

Your body can defend itself against serious threats

A bleeding wonder

Whatever else it can manage without, your body needs a good, steady and consistent supply of blood in order to survive and function properly. As we have already seen, it is the blood circulating round your body that provides your muscles with necessary supplies of food and oxygen. It is the blood that takes away the waste materials. It is the blood that ensures that such essential organs as your brain and kidneys are kept well fed. And it is the blood that enures that chemicals and hormones travel round the body quickly, efficiently and reliably. If for any reason the pump that circulates your blood stops working, or the supply of blood fails, then you will survive no more than a matter of minutes.

Naturally, the fact that the blood itself is a fluid and can easily be lost if the vessels which carry it are damaged means that the body has to have an effective and efficient system of ensuring that damage to the circulatory system does not result in a heavy leakage. There needs to be some sort of self-healing system.

And that is exactly what your body has!

Circulating in your blood, alongside the oxygen, the sugar, the vitamins, the hormones and the waste materials are some special proteins which, should they pass into damaged blood vessels, will automatically form a protective net. This net will catch blood cells and quickly form a clot which will seal the wound.

Not, of course, that the clotting mechanism which protects the blood supply is as simple as that. There are a whole host of fail-safe mechanisms which are designed to ensure that the system isn't accidentally triggered in to action when there is no leak and which ensure that the clotting system doesn't begin to operate until enough blood has flown through an injury site to wash away any dirt and bacteria which might be present.

Before a clot can form more than a dozen separate criteria must be satisfied!

Injury time

If you cut or injure yourself in any way, once the clotting mechanism has ensured that the amount of blood lost is kept to a minimum, another series of complex mechanisms will begin to ensure that any potential risk of infection is also kept to an absolute minimum.

As soon as a blood clot has formed and the loss of blood has been stopped, the damaged cells will release substances into the tissues resulting in the expansion of the local blood vessels and the flow of extra quantities of blood into the injury site. This additional blood will make the area red, swollen and hot. The heat will help damage any infective organisms and the swelling will ensure that the injured part is not used too much. By immobilising the area, the pain and stiffness will act as a natural splint.

White blood cells brought to the injury will help by swallowing up any debris or bacteria which might be there. These scavenging cells, bloated with rubbish, will allow themselves to be discharged from the body as pus once they have done their job. Once the debris has been cleared from the site and the scavenging cells have ensured that no infection remains, the injury will begin to heal.

It is at this point that the body shows an additional refinement, for the scar tissue it builds will be much tougher than the original area of skin that was damaged. Unsightly though it may be, the scar tissue ensures that the injured site is stronger than ever and better able to withstand any future injury.

Dying for a drink

Even if the blood-clotting mechanisms are not quick enough or powerful enough to cope with the damage done by a wound without there being an appreciable loss of fluid, all will not be lost. Your body still has a number of other mechanisms which will enable you to cope. Arteries supplying the injured area will constrict so as to limit further blood losses. Peripheral blood vessels supplying the skin will shut down so as to ensure that the supply of blood to the more essential organs can be preserved. The kidneys will cut the production of urine so that fluid levels within the body can be kept as high as possible. Fluids will be withdrawn from the tissue to dilate and increase the volume of the blood which remains. The red-blood-cell producing site within the body will step up production in order to replace the cells which have been lost. Finally, as an added refinement which any engineer would be proud of, the loss of blood will trigger off a thirst intended to ensure that the missing fluids are replaced as quickly as possible.

Fainting with purpose

If you lose quantities of blood or if your blood pressure suddenly falls, you will faint. When you faint you'll probably fall down flat.

This doesn't happen purely by chance. It is a deliberate trick employed by the body to ensure that your brain gets a good supply of blood. When you're standing, the blood has to travel upwards in order to reach the brain: if your blood volume is reduced, or if your blood pressure is low, the amount of blood getting to your brain is likely to be small. And since the brain is the nerve centre of the whole body, it doesn't like that. Blood brings oxygen and food and your brain needs a plentiful supply of both. The hormones that govern many activities within the body are produced by small glands within the skull. They

47

too need blood if they are to reach the rest of the body.

So you faint. Once you've fainted and you're lying flat the blood will be able to reach your brain far more easily. If the blood loss was relatively slight or the lowering of the blood pressure was temporary, you'll soon be able to sit up again.

Bedeviled kidneys

If you go out for the evening and drink several pints of fluid, your urine will become diluted. Instead of being its normal yellow colour it will be very pale. On the other hand, if you spend a hot day hiking across country and you drink very little fluid, your urine will be much darker.

As your consumption of fluid increases beyond your normal requirements your kidneys make the adjustments necessary in order to excrete the unwanted fluid. Similarly, after a long, dry hike your kidneys produce far more concentrated urine in order to compensate for the fact that your intake of fluid has been lower.

Your kidneys do not only have the job of maintaining your fluid balance at the right level. They are also responsible for ensuring that the salts, electrolytes and other essential chemicals in your body are kept balanced. Eat too much table salt and your kidneys will excrete the excess in your urine. Eat too little table salt and your kidneys will excrete no salt at all.

Battle stations

Although your body has a large number of automatic mechanisms which enable to to deal quickly and effectively with problems of all kinds, there are still some hazards which cannot be dealt with so readily. If, for example, you are lying half asleep in bed and you hear the sounds of an intruder wandering around downstairs, it is clear that you are going to have to take some sort of voluntary action. If you are walking along the street and a car mounts the pavement and heads straight for you, you are going to have to do something about the threat quickly.

In such situations you have to make a very fast decision and your body has to be ready to respond instantly. There may not ne any automatic reflex mechanisms to cope with these diverse threats, but what your body can do is prepare you for action.

To begin with, your body's sense organs suddenly become far more sensitive. It is obviously important that you should have as much information as possible about the threat. The pupils in your eyes dilate and your retinae become more sensitive to light. These twin actions mean that your vision will become more acute. At the same time your hearing will become sharper. Animals actually prick up their ears, though in humans this action has now been lost.

If you are in the dark, your head will turn so that your best ear gets the maximum amount of information. If you are outside in the light or in a room that is lit, your head will turn so that your eyes get the best possible view. Your muscles will tense and your whole body will be prepared to attempt to obtain the fullest data about the danger. Your breathing will stop for a moment or two and your heartbeat will temporarily slow down as you concentrate on looking and listening for vital clues.

While all this is going on, the pituitary gland, deep, inside your skull, will also be setting in motion a chain of events which will enable you to cope with the threat as efficiently as possible. The pituitary gland produces a hormone - the adrenocorticotrophic hormone - which stimulates the adrenal glands to produce steroids and adrenalin. Unless your sense organs recognise very quickly that the alarm was a false one, your whole body will soon be affected by the hormones produced by the adrenals.

The steroids and the adrenalin have a number of dramatic effects throughout your body. The flow of blood to your brain will increase so that you can make the best possible use of whatever brain tissue you have. The flow of blood to your skin will be drastically reduced. This latter effect has two uses: first it ensures that if you are injured the amount of blood lost will be kept to a minimum; second, it means that more blood will be available for supplying your brain and your muscles. When you turn pale with fright there are very good reasons for your pallor!

Acid will flow into your stomach to ensure that any food there is turned in to sugar as soon as possible. Your muscles will be tensed ready for action. Your heart rate will be increased so that the supply of blood to your essential organs is kept at a peak. Your respiratory rate will also be increased so that your lungs bring in plenty of oxygen. Your basal metabolic rate will also go up as your body starts to prepare itself for action.

No fleet at sea can reach battle stations as quickly as your body. All these defence mechanisms will enable you to defend yourself more effectively. If necessary you'll be able to fight for your life with a vigour you would never have thought possible. If running away is the best solution to your problems, then you'll be able to run faster than you've ever run before.

Untapped potential

Very few of us know the extent of our own strength. Only if we are pushed to our limits do we find out precisely what we can do.

Consider, for example, the case of the young mother whose daughter was trapped under the back wheel of a motor car. There were no strong men available to help rescue the child and the woman knew that by the time any lifting equipment arrived on the scene it would be too late. So she solved the problem herself. She lifted up the car and freed her daughter. Afterwards she was quite unable to believe what she'd managed to do. And she could no longer budge the car.

A more exotic tale reinforces the point. A zoologist working in Africa was alarmed to discover hyenas on his track: he realised that his only hope lay in trying to get off the ground and out of reach of the animals. So when he got close to a suitable tree he leapt upwards, clung to a branch and swung to safety. It was only when he came to climb down again a few hours later that he discovered he had jumped twelve feet into the air. When he finally did manage to get back down to earth he tried to jump into the tree again to see if he could do it. He couldn't get anywhere near the branch on which he had spent the night.

Such stories are relatively common. A 70-year-old Irish farmer woke to find his farmhouse on fire. Unable to escape in any other way, he climbed onto his roof and walked along a telegraph wire nine yards long. Then he climbed down the telegraph pole to the ground. He had never walked a tightrope in his life.

Finally, there is the account of a special agent who, during the Second World War, was travelling on a freighter when the ship was attacked by a German submarine. Having locked some important papers in the ship's safe, the agent single-handedly dragged the safe onto the deck so that it could be thrown overboard if the ship looked like being captured. The freighter survived, however, and when the attack was over the agent decided to return the safe to the captain's quarters. Without the fire in his arms and legs he couldn't budge the heavy object. It took four men to carry it back down again.

Few of us fulfil our physical or mental potential or succeed in harnessing the powers we have available within us.

Blowing hot and cold

Your body can only operate within a fairly narrow temperature range. If the temperature of your internal organs rises or falls more than a few degrees your ability to function and even to survive will be threatened. Although there are records of individuals having survived with exceptional body temperatures, it seems that most of us can only hope to remain alive if we succeed in keeping our internal body temperature above 30 degrees and below 45 degrees centigrade.

Since human beings are perfectly capable of existing in environments where the outside temperatures are well outside this range it is clear that there must be some sort of thermostat inside the body which operates independently and which uses internal mechanisms to preserve a suitable internal temperature. These internal mechanisms are very adaptable. They work as effectively for the Eskimo living in his igloo as they do for the Arab wandering through the blistering heat of the desert. In both situations the body maintains its stable, internal temperature by modifying its physical structure to suit the demands of the external environment.

If, for example, you are suddenly snatched out of your armchair and deposited in a deckchair on a sunny beach a number of mechanisms will switch on automatically and produce clearly recordable changes in your body structure.

The first thing you'll notice will be the dilation of your surface blood vessels. Your skin will go pink because a greater quantity of blood will be flowing near the surface. This increase in superficial blood flow will enable your body to get rid of heat simply through the fact that the blood will lose the heat to the surrounding air.

Even more heat will be lost by your body's cunning use of the fact that when water evaporates heat is lost. People who live in very hot climates but who do not have refrigerators have for centuries kept their butter cool by storing it in water-filled porous pots which allow water to evaporate. Your body uses the same technique. When sweat evaporates from your skin, heat is lost into the surrounding air.

Clearly, this sudden and sometimes dramatic increase in the amount of fluid being lost by the body could lead to a dangerous amount of dehydration. Consequently, when you sweat automatically operated mechanisms ensure that you produce less urine. In addition, as the sweat pours out so the amount of saliva you produce will fall, thus making your mouth dry. And so you'll get thirsty and drink more fluids.

Other mechanisms come into play too. Since human bodies generate far less heat when they do little exercise, you'll probably find yourself feeling lethargic when you're hot. Your lethargy will stop you running round so that your own heat production will be kept to a minimum. Finally, you may also notice that your rate of breathing will increase. Since you lose heat when you breathe out, this is another way of keeping your body temperature down.

All these mechanisms will be brought in to action if you find yourself sitting on a hot beach. But consider what will happen if you are whisked from there to a snowy ski slope in Austria.

You'll stop sweating, of course, and your breathing rate will go down, too. You'll also turn rather pale as those superficial blood vessels shut down in order to ensure that the amount of heat lost through the skin is kept to an absolute minimum. Because muscle activity actually produces more heat, you may also find yourself shivering. You may stamp your feet in an automatic attempt to produce some internal warmth. Finally, you'll probably notice that some of the small hairs on your body will stand on end, producing what are commonly known as goose pimples. This mechanism is a leftover from the days when we were all covered in a thick hairy coat; by standing on end the hairs could keep a layer of warm air trapped next to the skin.

Safety margins

Your body is well prepared for disaster. You may lose nearly three quarters of your lung, liver or kidney tissue without noticing any substantive loss of function. You've got a similar an=mount of heart muscle in reserve too. And you can afford to lose yards of intestine without any appreciable effect on your digestion.

All this spare tissue allows your body to cope with exceptional demands. Your heart may beat at a rate of something around 60-70 times a minute during normal circumstances, but in a crisis it will be well able to beat over 150 times a minute. Your body can get by with just a few litres of air going into your lungs every minute. In a crisis your body and your lungs can bring in and deal with over one hundred litres of air a minute.

Tears with feeling

A few years ago, when some car manufacturers started fitting their car headlights with washer and wiper blades, many people applauded the daring and originality of the concept.

In fact, of course, those manufacturers were merely imitating something that your body does far more efficiently. Without you even being aware of it, your body pumps a steady flow of tears over the surface of your eyes in order to wash away impurities. At the same time, your eyelids blink unceasingly in order to wipe the eyes clean.

If the eyes are threatened by a foreign object of any kind the system goes into overdrive. If a speck of grit or a small fly finds its way into one of your eyes, for example, a sophisticated defence system will immediately swing into action. Tears will flood across the eye in an attempt to wash the irritant away and your eyelids will temporarily go into spasm in an attempt to protect the eye from any further damage.

We only become fully aware of the importance and efficiency of this system when anything goes wrong. Thus, if for any reason your eyelids are paralysed and cannot function normally, there will be a real risk that your eye surfaces will become damaged and ulcerated.

There are mechanisms to protect you against disease and infection

Hot but not bothered

When a patient has a high temperature, the doctor will probably prescribe a drug intended to bring the temperature down. However, there is now evidence which strongly suggests that there is a good explanation for the fact that people who are ill often have a fever. When we have an infection our bodies deliberately raise our tissue temperature in order to help us cope more effectively with the threat. The increase in temperature seems to improve the capacity of the body's defence mechanisms, while at the same time it threatens the invading organisms. It is known that bacteria are more likely to die when the temperature changes and that they are particularly susceptible when the temperature goes up.

The mechanism can go wrong, of course. Occasionally, body temperature rises far too rapidly and goes far too high. Nevertheless, it seems that a fever isn't necessarily a bad thing.

Starve a fever

Patients who have high temperatures as a result of internal infections usually lose their appetites. And according to Dr George Mann of Vanderbilt University in Nashville, Tennessee, there is good reason for this. Dr Mann argues that when someone with an infection and a fever loses his appetite he is unconsciously but deliberately starving the organisms which have caused the infection.

Dr Mann claims that, whereas the human body can survive quite well on its own stored supplies, the bacteria which cause infections need ingested food in order to survive. There is certainly evidence to support this theory. It is known, for example, that during periods of famine people normally susceptible to malaria seem to acquire an inexplicable immunity to the disease.

Some physicians with more faith in high-level technology than in old wives' tales may find this slightly disturbing. It does, after all, give credence to the saying which suggests that `it is wise to starve a fever'. Incidentally, it seems possible that the loss of appetite which occurs in other diseases may merit the same explanation. It is, for example, commonly known that cancer sufferers lose their appetite, and this loss of appetite may be designed to weaken the multiplying cancer cells.

Spit and polish

If you have ever had a bad infection of your chest, you'll have noticed that you produce large quantities of phlegm. Your doctor will have encouraged you to cough up the sputum and to spit it out.

You may have thought that the stuff you produced under these circumstances was rather unpleasant and you may have found yourself reluctant to take his advice. What you probably haven't realised is that the phlegm is a very important part of your body's defence mechanism.

When the respiratory tract is infected, some of the cells which line it step up their production of a special type of sticky mucus. Other cells, which have tiny bristles, then move the mucus up the tubes of your lungs towards your mouth. As the sticky mucus travels, it picks up bacteria and pollutants of all kinds. That's why it sometimes comes out looking green, yellow, brown or black.

When you cough up the mucus and spit it out you're doing just what your body wants you to do.

If the tiny mucus-producing cells and the small bristle-bearing cells become very irritated (as they do by continued exposure to cigarette smoke, for example) they can be paralysed. It is because these cells get paralysed that smokers are so prone to infections of the chest.

A life-saving nuisance

When we develop a cough most of us do our best to get rid of it with the aid of sweets and linctuses. Although that is understandable, since coughs are something of a nuisance, it is worth remembering that the cough reflex is one of the most important reflexes in the whole of your body. If the reflex wasn't there, you would choke to death if you ever accidentally got a piece of food stuck in your windpipe. And if you ever got a minor infection of your chest heavy enough to increase the output from the mucus-producing cells in your lungs, you'd risk being drowned by your secretions. Any doctor will confirm that far more people have died from not being able to cough than have done so from coughing

The coughing mechanism is delightfully simple. The larynx narrows so that the air coming out of the lungs is put under pressure. When the pressure is great enough the larynx suddenly relaxes and there is an explosion of air out of the lungs. Anything stuck in or above the larynx will be blown out and the danger will be over.

That, at least, is what happens when you have a real cough. The annoying little half-hearted cough that hangs on after a cold is often more of a habit than a genuine, full-blooded laryngeal explosion.

Still, now you know why the cough is there, you might perhaps be a little less upset next time you have an explosion or two of your own!

Up, up and away

If you eat something that is badly infected and likely to prove a threat to your body, messages will very quickly be sent to a special centre in your brain. From there more messages will go to nerves which supply your diaphragm and to nerves which supply the muscles of your abdomen. Muscles which are normally used exclusively for breathing will temporarily be borrowed too. The result of all this activity will be that - very shortly after the offending material has been swallowed - your diaphragm will press down and your abdominal muscles will press in. Your stomach, caught in between these two powerful sets of muscles, will be under a tremendous amount of pressure. And any food still left in your stomach will be forcibly ejected at great speed.

In short, you will vomit.

As an added precaution, there is another mechanism designed to deal with any infected material which has found its way into the rest of your gastro-intestinal tract. Should the infected matter manage to get past the stomach and travel further, into the large bowel, a fresh set of mechanisms will ensure that the material is moved out of the other end of the tract as quickly as possible.

You'll develop diarrhoea.

Either way, your body is well equipped to deal with infections that get in through your mouth!

Secret allies

It is very well known that men are men and women are women because of the distribution of sex hormones within their bodies. When a teenage girl's production of progesterone and oestrogen rises, she will start to develop all the outward signs of womanhood. Her breasts will swell and her hips flare; she will start to ovulate and she'll start to menstruate. When a boy's production of testosterone begins to build up, he will acquire broader shoulders, hair on his face and chest and a deeper voice.

What is perhaps less well known, however, is the fact that these very basic hormonally induced changes are not as simple as they might appear to be. There are, in fact, a number of subtleties, designed to ensure not only that men find women attractive and that women find men attractive, but also that the survival of the species is guaranteed.

As a single example, consider the vaginal secretions which are produced when a young girl begins to show sign of sexual maturity and which will continue in varying degrees of abundance until she ceases to be fertile. These secretions will, of course, increase when the woman is aroused in order to make penetration easier and more comfortable, but there is an additional, delightfully sophisticated touch which ensures that during a woman's fertile years her vagina has some protection against infection.

At and after puberty the vaginal walls secrete glycogen, which is broken down by local bacteria to produce an acid. This acid ensures that foreign bacteria (most of which cannot survive in an acid environment) find the vagina inhospitable. Consequently, when the woman becomes pregnant the foetus she carries is unlikely to be exposed to any maternal infection.

Glycogen production continues throughout a woman's fertile years and stops automatically when she is no longer likely to conceive.

Sex hormones do not merely ensure that men and women enjoy each other. They also help ensure that their pleasure is fruitful.

Your body can develop self-protective symptoms

The importance of pain

A few years ago a doctor working in a leper colony was trying to open a door which had stuck. A twelve year old boy saw him struggling. To the doctor's surprise, the young boy - a leper - succeeded in opening the door without any effort. The key, which had been too stiff for the healthy doctor to turn, proved no barrier to the boy.

It was only when the door was standing open that the doctor noticed the boy's hand. It was cut and bleeding where the key had dug into the flesh. Because leprosy attacks and kills the nerve endings, the boy had not felt any pain when he had turned the key. And without the presence of pain to restrict his movement, he had been able to exert pressure in a way that no healthy individual would have been able to endure.

This small incident was important, for the doctor realised that lepers lose parts of their bodies not because the disease eats away at the flesh (as had been suspected) but because, with the sensation of pain gone, the tissues can easily be damaged. Lepers commonly lose fingers and toes and, before the incident with the key, it had been thought that the digits disappear simply through some direct action of the bacillus leprae. In fact, the damage indirectly resulted from the absence of any pain defence mechanisms. The doctor even found that some lepers lost their fingers during the night simply because they didn't feel the rats nibbling away at their flesh.

It isn't only those suffering from leprosy who have to endure life without pain. Some people are unlucky enough to be born without the necessary parts of their nervous systems. They, too, quickly discover that pain has many uses. For example, one young woman born without any pain receptors suffered terribly from badly damaged bones and joints. Because she didn't feel any pain or discomfort, she never moved when she was sitting uncomfortably or when she was lying in a position which put an unnatural strain on her skeleton. She became a cripple simply because her body couldn't use pain to help it stay healthy.

You and I might find the idea of life without pain attractive. But it can be truly unbearable. If you or I pick up something hot by mistake the pain we feel will ensure that we drop it again quickly. Someone without any pain sensation who picks up something hot will keep on holding it until their flesh begins to sizzle. If you or I get into a bath filled with water that is too hot, we'll quickly jump out again. If an individual who has no pain nerve endings makes the same mistake, he'll suffer severe burns. If you or I shut a finger in the door we'll speedily open the door again. The painless individual will push on the door to shut it. If you or I walk into a sandstorm our eyelids will protect our eyes. The man or woman who feels no pain will end up with badly damaged eyes. If you or I cut through a piece of wood and start to slice into a limb by mistake we'll soon stop. The man who doesn't feel pain will lose his limb.

Pain may be something of a nuisance and it may be something that most of us feel we would gladly do without, but those unhappy individuals who have no capacity to feel it would cheerfully exchange places with us. Without the defences afforded by the sensation of pain, most of those whom we would envy spend much of their lives in hospital. Few live very long.

There are even mechanisms to help you overrule inappropriate mechanisms

The automatic aspirin

Pain plays an important part in the defence of our bodies. And yet there are, of course, many times when the pain we experience is of little value. When a pain tells us that something is damaging our bodies we can use it as a warning sign. We can pull away from whatever it is that is doing the damage. But the pain will sometimes continue even when we've done everything we can to ensure that no further damage is done. And that type of pain can be both uncomfortable and useless. Indeed, it may even damage us further by weakening our will to live.

However, do not imagine that your body is unaware of the fact that the pain sensations it produces are sometimes debilitating. On the contrary, your body has another system designed specifically to help cope with pain. A separate system is used since the body is thereby provided both with additional flexibility and with an opportunity to maintain the pain sensory endings in a very sensitive state.

The existence of this additional mechanism was first suspected when an army physician noticed that men who had been severely injured often needed only very small doses of pain-relieving drugs. It was also discovered that in many instances quite severe pain could be relieved by tablets and injections with no active pharmacological ingredients.

Now, the existence of something called the placebo effect had been well known since the beginning of the nineteenth century. Traditionally, many doctors had used tablets containing nothing more than starch or lactose in an attempt to obtain some psychological healing effect. The experiences of the Second World War, however, inspired researchers to begin to investigate the whole subject of placebos more closely. Some intriguing results quickly began to appear in the medical journals.

In 1946 Jellineck found that, out of 199 patients who complained of having a headache, no less than 120 got relief from using a placebo. No less than 15 other studies, on a total of 1082 patients, showed that placebos have an effectiveness of something like 35 per cent when given to patients with pains. It was also found that the appearance of the placebo has an effect - in the Journal of Mental Science in 1957 Trouton wrote that, for medical purposes, placebos work best if they are red, yellow or brown in colour, bitter in flavour and either very large or very small. Surgeons discovered that if they opened up patients who had been suffering from angina (chest pain caused by heart disease) and then simply sewed up the wounds again, their patients would make marvellous progress if they were told that they had had bypass surgery. Researchers even found that many patients who take placebos and benefit from them also suffer from the sort of side-effects that are normally associated with active drugs. In the Journal of the American Medical Association in 1955 Beecher reported no less than 35 different toxic effects suffered by patients taking placebos. In Medical Times in 1963 Pogge noted 38 different types of side-effect. Patients were reported to have become addicted to placebo tablets which contained no active constituents at all.

Many scientists struggled hard to explain all this. Some physicians, puzzled but impressed by the placebo response, seemed convinced that these dummy tablets were working simply because they had a psychological effect on the people who took them. Psychiatrists and psychologists tried to analyse the type of individual likely to respond best to placebos, but they were unable to find any pattern. The only certain factor that could be identified was faith, which seemed to be a vital ingredient. If the patient believed that the placebo would help, then it probably would. If he didn't believe, then there would probably be no useful effect. A placebo offered by an unenthusiastic nurse had only a 25 per cent response rate. The same placebo offered by an enthusiastic doctor gave success in 70 per cent of cases.

It has been discovered that the placebo response can be explained by physiological activity within the body, rather than by some mysterious and unexplained psychological status. Researchers working in laboratories around the world have become interested in opiate-like chemicals found in the brain. Called endorphins, these chemicals have extraordinary properties. In an article in The Lancet in 1978, Jon D. Levine, Newton C. Gordon and Howard

L. Fields of the Departments of Neurology, Physiology and Oral Surgery, respectively, at the University of California in San Francisco not only suggested that the pain-relieving response produced by placebos is generated by the release of endorphins but pointed out that the pain-relieving mechanisms through which morphine and placebos work seem to be similar. They made three observations which supported this association:

1 With repeated use over long periods the pain relief produced by placebos tends to become less effective.

2 Patients using placebos tend to use larger amounts as time goes by.

3 When the placebo is withdrawn patients often show signs of distress.

All these problems are also associated with the use of opiates such as morphine.

Levine, Gordon and Fields argued that, if the type of pain relief that patients obtain with placebos is controlled with endorphins, then an opiate antagonist, normally used to block morphine, should block the placebo effect. The three researchers studies 51 patients, all of whom had impacted wisdom teeth. The results confirmed their hypothesis. As they had suspected, the patients who received the placebo obtained pain relief until they were given the morphine antagonist.

The precise pathways through which this pain-relieving system works are still a mystery. It seems likely that the release of the endorphin, the internal pain reliever, can be triggered by faith and belief. But is seems that there is also an overriding device of outstanding ingenuity which is set to operate when the production of pain, normally a protective mechanism, is likely to put the organism at greater risk than might otherwise be the case.

As I have already explained, feeling pain is often vital to our safety. Normally if you sprain or break your ankle the pain that is produced will stop you walking on it. If you walked on the damaged limb and used the damaged bones and ligaments, you would run the risk of doing permanent harm. The pain protects those structures. However, there are certain circumstances when you would be better off using the damaged limb and risking further damage to it. If, for example, you had twisted your ankle running away from a mugger, you would be in greater danger if you sat down and rested your leg than if you continued to run.

It seems that if the whole organism is threatened, the brain can trigger the release of specific types of endorphin which will dull and override the effect of the pain and enable the individual to use the wounded part of his body. It seems very likely that this release of a pain-suppressing endorphin is triggered when stress levels within the body reach a peak. If so, this phenomenon explains why sportsmen who are injured in important games can often manage to carry on playing with injuries which might normally have crippled them.

A labour-saving device

According to Dr Alan Gintzler of the Department of Anatomy at Columbia University, it seems possible that endorphins help women to endure pain during labour. Gintzler has shown that pain threshold and pain tolerance levels are increased during the final days of pregnancy by an automatic increase in the production of endorphins. The survival of the individual organism may not be threatened by the pains of labour, but the survival of the species could be at risk if pregnancy were too uncomfortable an experience. And so nature intervenes with a painkiller.

Or perhaps that is too cynical an explanation. Could it simply be that Mother Nature has decided to show her sense of sympathy for the pregnant woman in a practical way?

Cold comfort

A few years ago a Dutch professor described with some astonishment and a little pride hoe he had begun to suffer the early signs of a cold just before he was to give an important lecture but had succeeded in suppressing those symptoms until the lecture was over. He readily admitted that once he had completed his engagement the sore throat, stuffy nose and headache returned.

I myself had a very similar experience recently when I found myself suffering from the early symptoms of a heavy cold a short while before I was due to spend two weeks touring the country to promote a book. The plans included several dozen television and radio appearances during that time and I was very conscious of the fact that I would not be able to do the book justice if I was sitting in the studios blowing my nose, coughing and spluttering all the time. Without any conscious effort on my part the cold symptoms disappeared and stayed away for the while fortnight. They returned the day after I finished the tour. As soon as my defence mechanisms relaxed, the virus, which had obviously been lying vanquished but undefeated, came out of hiding.

We all have within us defence mechanisms if this kind which can be mobilised in emergencies.

Mind over matter

It has long been suspected that the human brain can influence the body in ways that we do not understand. Research has shown that genuine physical responses within the body can be controlled by the brain. There is evidence that automatic reflexes which were previously regarded as being quite outside voluntary control can be stopped or started by conscious effort.

For example, it seems that the digestive process can be specifically controlled. If you eat a very fatty meal your body will normally produce special enzymes which will break down the fat and turn it into products which can be transported in the blood. It is now know, however, that the production of these special fat-dissolving enzymes can be consciously controlled. Concentrate hard enough and you can force your body to produce fat-dissolving enzymes even if you haven't eaten any fat.

Even more startling, perhaps, the body's immune system, previously regarded as an entirely automatic phenomenon, can also be voluntarily controlled under some circumstances. It has been shown, for example, that the body's response to the type of intradermal tuberculin injection used in the Mantoux test for T.B. immunity can be influenced by hypnosis. Normally such an injection will produce a response from the body's own defences. A swelling and a small red mark will develop at the site of the injection if the body has been previously exposed to tuberculosis and has been able to prepare defences. Such a response can, however, be overruled if a subject under hypnosis, who would have reacted to the injection, is told that he will not respond. Surprisingly, it seems that even a cell-mediated immunity reaction may be controlled by the mind.

We still don't understand the extent of the mind's power over the body and nor do we understand why there should be such power. All we can say for certain is that the mind does have power over the body in very many different ways.

If a man is told that he is at the North Pole and he believes what he is told, he'll show physical signs which suggest that his body is reacting as though he were at the North Pole. He'll go pale and shiver. If a hay fever sufferer is shown a photograph of the sort of plant to which he is allergic, he'll sneeze. When the film Lawrence of Arabia was shown, cinema managers around the world reported that the sales of ice cream rocketed. The endless desert scenes had made the patrons feel uncomfortably hot.

Hypnotists use the power of the mind over the body in order to exert their influence. The operator must only convince the patient that something is true and the patient will act accordingly. If he convinces the patient that his arms are as heavy as lead, then the patient will be unable to lift his arms. If he convinces the patient that a piece of ice is a red hot poker and he then touched the patient's skin with the ice a blister will develop. The body will react to the suggestion, and not to the reality, and signs of a genuine burn will appear.

The final dignity

When life is artificially prolonged, pain and distress are only too common. People who die natural deaths, however, do not usually suffer any considerable pain or discomfort as death approaches. When medical intervention is kept to a minimum the body usually ensures that the final hours and days are as peaceful as possible. Pain-relieving endorphins are secreted automatically and the individual drifts slowly, almost contentedly, into an unconscious state.

And there are mechanisms which lie half forgotten and unused...

Show me the way to go home

Every year thousands of birds who are only a few months old manage to fly hundreds of miles in order to spend the winter in a warmer country. They fly without maps and without any artificial navigational aids.They fly across the oceans where there are no landmarks. And yet they invariably reach their destinations safely. Then, as the seasons change once more, they fly all the way back again. Similarly, newspapers often contain stories about family pets which have got lost but which have, nevertheless, managed to travel long distances in order to find their way back home.

No one seems to know precisely how birds and animals manage to navigate so accurately, but most scientists now argue that birds use some sort of inbuilt compass to help them follow the earth's magnetic fields.

Since creatures which most of us regard as less intelligent than ourselves seem to be able to navigate very well without instruments, might we assume that, although most of us have lost the knack, we too have some sort of inbuilt system which is designed to help us find our way around the world?

The evidence suggests so. Most dramatic of all was the work done by a British researcher. Working with students whom he blindfolded, Dr Robin Baker of Manchester showed not only that they were able to point their way back to their starting point, even when they had been taken on a confusing and deliberately circuitous route, but that they were unable to do this with magnetic-field-inducing coils on their heads.

Not that this startling experiment would have been much of a surprise for one of the world's greatest explorers. Captain Cook, the famous British sea captain and explorer, took a Polynesian with him on at least one of his journeys: according to Cook the man could always point accurately towards his own home island without any obvious external aids.

Thanks for the memory

Human memory is a very strange thing. In some ways it is very efficient. Numerous psychologists have tried to assess the power of the human brain to retain information and innumerable mnemonists have been studied by experts who have tried to find out why some memories are better than others. Consequently, we do at least know a little about the human memory and about how it can be improved.

Some of the most illuminating research was done by Professor A.R. Luria, a Russian psychologist who spent years working with Solomon Veniaminoff, one of the most remarkable memory men of all time.

Luria has described how Veniaminoff used to put things that he wanted to remember in an imaginary street, giving each a special place that he would construct specifically. So, for example, one object would be in a doorway, another would be in the gutter, a third would be leaning against a fire hydrant. To remember the object, Veniaminoff would simply take an imaginary walk down his imaginary street.

To remember numbers or to perform calculations, Veniaminoff used to draw a blackboard in his mind. And to forget things he would rub them off the blackboard. Since he was an exception, however, other researchers have tried to find out more about how the average memory works. In the process, they've observed all sorts of remarkable phenomena which we are sometimes prone to take for granted.

They have found, for example, that different people seem able to remember things in different ways. Wine tasters store the memory of the taste of scores of wines. Art historians store images. Musicians retain scores and arrangements in their minds. Tailors retain the `feel' of types of cloth. Some people remember types of smell. We can all retain muscle movement memories (if you learned how to ride a bicycle when you were a child, you'll still be able to ride a bicycle). In addition to verbal, visual and motor memories, we store emotions too. Certain things bring tears to our eyes because they bring back sad memories. And some things make us smile.

The research indicates that you'll probably remember better if you don't try too hard. You may be able to store a visual memory more effectively if you close your eyes as soon as the picture you want to retain begins to fade. By doing so you'll keep the image on your retina and your imagination will then help. You're also more likely to remember things if you return to the place where you learnt them.

It has been shown that when divers are debriefed much better information is obtained if they are debriefed under water. Could that explain why sports teams often do better when playing at home, where they have been trained? Could it be that schoolchildren who take examinations in rooms where they have studied have an inbuilt advantage?

There is evidence, too, to show that a slight amount of stress will improve the memory. A severe shock can produce total amnesia. A little pressure can help an individual retain a memory.

And, finally, sometimes it appears that our memories absorb information without our being aware of it. Patients who have been under total anaesthesia have been able to recall words and snatches of conversation between the surgeons.

Second sight

Much of what we see is never consciously registered by our brains. If subliminal messages are flashed onto TV or cinema screens the messages will register with our subconscious minds only. Researchers have shown that aircrew members taught to press buttons when they have spotted enemy aircraft will sometimes press them when the aircraft have been there but they have not knowingly seen them. The unconscious ability to see is, it seems, sometimes stronger than its conscious counterpart.

To illustrate this point an experiment was organised in which individuals watching nonsense words being projected onto a cinema screen were given shocks when certain words were shown. Predictably, the experiment showed that the volunteers exhibited the same sort of responses as Pavlov's dogs. They began to show physical signs of fear every time they saw a word which would by accompanied by a shock.

What these researchers also revealed, however, was that when words which should have been associated with electrical shocks by the volunteers were falsely identified by their conscious minds their bodies nevertheless responded accurately, unconsciously making correct identifications.

And if that doesn't impress you, consider this: a boy who was taught to blink when he someone say the number ten also began to blink when he heard people say sums, the answers to which were ten. Thus he would automatically blink when he heard the numbers 92-82, 65-55 and so on. Somehow the automatic reflex he had acquired had linked into a part of his brain that was capable of doing small sums.

Whatever else we may suspect about our eyesight we do know now that we have a lot to learn. Could it be, for example, that when we act on impulse, or have a hunch about something, we are using information that has been fed into our brains without our knowledge?

Things aren't what they seem

Appearances can often be very deceptive. If you've put a straight stick into a pond and watched it suddenly appear to bend you'll be interested to hear about some experiments first tried in the early 1930s and long since forgotten.

Reporting his work in the Journal of Experimental Psychology in 1933, J.J. Gibson described how he conducted some investigations with prism spectacles which were designed to make vertical straight lines appear curved. He noticed early on that after a while the lines seemed less and less curved and he decided to investigate this process of adaptation to find out how the eyes could overcome the effect of the prism.

In the course of finding out about the phenomenon he discovered that if a straight stick looked curved to someone wearing prism spectacles then it would also feel curved. He found that people who wore the distorting spectacles and then ran their hands down a solid door frame would be convinced that the door frame had a bend in it. He decided that this implied that visual perception must be matched by an accommodating sense of kinesthetic perception. Or, to translate, that the person wearing the prism spectacles imagines that his arm has moved in the way that his eyes have told him it should move.

In a Journal of Experimental Psychology monograph published in 1967 by the American Psychological Association, Leon Festinger, Hirosho Ono, Clarke A. Burnham and Donald Bamber described experimental work which confirmed this theory. It seems that the feedback we get from our muscles can indeed be overpowered by the imaginary feedback we think we ought to be getting according to the visual input our eyes are providing.

Like so many other surprising discoveries it is difficult to judge the precise significance of this conclusion. Its immediate value lies in its vivid illustration of the extent of the power of the mind over the body.

The sixth sense

Scientists tend to greet all new ideas and partly substantiated theories with a mixture of scepticism and fear. If the ideas put forward have been tainted with the smell of commercial exploitation, then the scepticism and fear will be even stronger. To a certain extent that is a healthy response, but if new ideas also conflict with what are considered solid scientific facts, there is a danger that unavoidable and incontrovertible truths will be denied simply because they do not fit in with well-established theories. When this happens, prejudice replaces scientific judgement and superstitions retain precedence over evidence.

Such a pattern I am afraid, is exactly what has been revealed whenever the question of the existence of a sixth sense has been raised. Scientists argue that since the concept of a sixth sense is something of a musical-hall joke and since the theoretical support for the reality of any such phenomenon would undermine a number of carefully structured manmade scientific truths, the theory must be invalid.

In my view, there is now an overpowering amount of evidence to support the theory that a sixth sense does exist and that such things as extrasensory perception, telepathy, and premonitions are as real as vision and hearing. The capacities of the sense organs we know about are far greater than we might have suspected a few years ago. The capacities of the sense organs we have not yet identified are so vast that it is probably unwise at this stage even to make an attempt to define any boundaries.

One of the reasons why scientists have been so suspicious of claims which apparently show the paranormal capacities of the mind has undoubtedly been the fact that there has for many years been a certain eccentricity about many of the individuals working in this field. The uncritical work which has been published has often been subjective and presented in a style more appropriate for romantic fiction that straightforward scientific reporting. It is perhaps not surprising that scientists reared on a diet of double-bind trials and carefully planned laboratory experiments should remain unconvinced when evidence offered during television talk shows undeniable proof of the existence of a paranormal force.

Recently, however, much more solid scientific work has shown beyond any reasonable doubt that the human brain does have abilities which physiologists cannot yet properly explain. Laboratory experiments around the world indicate that some people can project and receive information. Researchers are even beginning to find possible explanations. Dr Peter Fenwick and his colleagues at The Maudsley Hospital in London have found significant numbers of head injuries, episodes of being knocked unconscious, blackouts and serious illnesses in the medical histories of the mediums they have studied. From their work it seems that there is a link between an individual being knocked unconscious and that individual later showing such skills as telepathy or clairvoyance.

Unless there is a major international conspiracy to mislead and confuse us all, we can no longer ignore the strength of this evidence. Whether orthodox physicians like it or not, it seems that human beings have the capacity to affect matter by the power of the mind alone. The fact that we do not understand precisely how these mechanisms operate can no longer be used as evidence that they do not exist.

Sound sense

Have you ever noticed that if you are at a party where dozens of people are talking loudly and someone mentions your name, your ears will automatically prick up? You will have isolated the sounds of your name from the general hubbub even though you hadn't been consciously listening to the conversation concerned.

Well, it seems that our hearing acuity is indeed very much more powerful than any of us might have imagined. In one fascinating piece of research, volunteers listened to various numbers being read out on a piece of recording tape. Every time the number five was mentioned, a puff of air was blown onto the eyelids of the volunteers. Eventually, the individuals all acquired reflexes which meant that they blinked whenever they heard the number five on the tape.

That was straightforward enough. But the next part of the research was really remarkable. For the people who had organised the experiment discovered that when they turned down the tape recorder and played it so that the voice on it was inaudible, the volunteers still blinked every time the number five was mentioned.

Somehow they had managed to hear unconsciously what they had been unable to detect consciously.

The sweet smell of success

Most of us have learned to be ashamed of our bodily odours. And yet there is considerable evidence to show that our individual smells have a power and purpose of their own. Many different creatures use specific pheromones to help them mark the extent of their own personal territory, to warn others of impending dangers and to establish pecking orders. Man is no different.

Anthropologist Louis Leakey has been reported as having suggested that body odour was an important human defence mechanism in the days when man was likely to be eaten on the way back from hunting trips. The smell put off most predators. A psychologist at the University of Chicago has shown that women who live together tend to acquire menstrual patterns which match. A researcher at San Francisco State University has produced evidence which suggests that the pattern of a woman's menstrual cycle is influenced by the odours of the women around her. I described this last phenomenon in a recent book and when touring to promote the paperback edition I was told by women producers, presenters, researchers and secretaries everywhere that they had noticed it. It isn't always easy to know why certain physiological mechanisms exist, but the actual evidence for their existence is sometimes readily available.

Perhaps most remarkable (and easily explained) of all is the evidence we now have which shows that some human smells have a genuine sexual value. It has been known since the 1940s that animals produce substances which have a strong stimulating effect on members of the opposite sex. Women can be attracted to seats which have been sprayed with sexually stimulating pheromones and men can be artificially induced to find photographs of women sexually appealing. Researchers have even been able to show that while secretions from the vagina of a non-ovulating woman are rated as bland or mildly unpleasant by men, secretions taken from thr vagina of an ovulating woman are rated as definitely pleasant.

The food of love

If you're the sort of person who is always falling in an out of love and who tends to get very depressed when a love affair comes to an end, the chances are that your problems are linked to the amount of phenylethylamine in your brain.

This naturally occurring substance, structurally rather similar to amphetamines, is thought to be the chemical responsible for the highs and lows of being in love. According to Dr David Schwartz, Dr Michael Liebowitz and Dr Donald Klein of the New York State Psychiatric Institute, people whose production of phenylethylamine is disordered fall in love very quickly and then, if they are rejected, tend to go into a deeper decline.

When they are in love they experience a high which is similar to the sort of intense pleasure that people experience when they're taking amphetamines. When they are in a low mood they have symptoms which are said to be similar to those exhibited by people when they have suddenly stopped using such stimulants. They sleep too much, eat too much and are unable to get on with the normal business of living.

What makes the whole subject even more fascinating is the fact that the only food which contains phenylethylamine in high quantities is chocolate. And very emotional people will often admit that they tend to gorge themselves on chocolate when they're feeling low.

Could it be that this craving for something sweet is simply a sign that the brain is looking for an answer to its own problems?

A natural Valium

Benzodiazepines, such as Librium and Valium, were first introduced into medical practice in the 1960s. Since then these drugs have become more and more popular in many countries of the world. Thousands of tons of benzodiazepines are consumed annually. Many researchers produced evidence to show that the drugs in this group have a sedating and calming effect on human beings, but no one really knew how they worked until the late 1970s.

Then, through research by Richard Squires (of the pharmaceutical company Ferrosan) and Claus Braestrup (of the St Hans Mental Hospital in Roskilde, Denmark), it became clear that the benzodiazepines work because they have an effect on specific receptors which exist within the brain. These receptors seem to be formulated in such a way that they can respond only to drugs like Valium. And if a benzodiazepine receptor occurs within the brain, there must also be some sort of natural benzodiazepine to use that receptor.

So far scientists have been unable to identify with any certainty the natural chemical which has an effect like Valium. But it seems reasonable to assume that individuals who suffer unduly from anxiety do so because their natural production of this automatic Valium is inadequate. Or, perhaps, because their exposure to stress and pressure is so great that their internal production of `Valium' cannot keep up.

PART 2: INTERVENTION

It should be clear by now that our bodies are remarkably capable of looking after themselves.

And yet few of us take advantage of these self-healing mechanisms and protective capabilities. In this section I'm going to look at some of the ways in which we deal with our bodies when things go wrong and investigate the strengths and weaknesses of the interventionist techniques we favour.

The Interventionist Approach

Interventionist medicine can be divided into three parts:

- orthodox medical care

- alternative medical remedies

- home treatments

On the pages which follow I want to explain why intervention can be dangerous.

Blinkers can impede your vision

Doctors have always been suspicious of anything new and often reluctant to listen to theories and ideas which contradict traditional attitudes. From Paracelsus to Lind and from Semmelweiss to Freud, medical history is littered with doctors who have learned that the medical establishment does not take kindly to original ideas or to new concepts which threaten the status quo. Medical students are taught that they should avoid asking uncomfortable questions and young doctors who wish to succeed must eschew the unconventional and remain unquestioningly faithful to the established truths. Any physician who rocks the boat, makes waves or swim against the tide will soon find himself floundering in deep water - and struggling to survive! To be successful a physician must respect the prejudices of his elders, adhere to the dogma of his teachers and shut his mind to theories which do not fit in with orthodox medical doctrines. Medicine is an unstructured discipline in which uncertainty, confusion and ignorance are too often disguised with conceit, arrogance and bigotry.

At a time when the half-life of medical information is shrinking and the limits of traditional, interventionist medicine are daily becoming more and more apparent, this ostrich-type behaviour is difficult to understand and impossible to justify. Unless doctors are prepared to consider the unexpected, the unlikely and even the apparent;y impossible, patients will do well to regard rigidly orthodox interventionists with a certain amount of suspicion and cynicism.

Doctors under the influence

Orthodox medical practice is big business. There are thousands of companies which have a vested interest in your ill-health. Tere are instrument makers, drug companies, private hospitals and insurance brokers. For every nurse and every doctor offering practical health and advice, there are countless administrators and clerks helping to ensure that the medical machine continues to whirr away profitably.

The fact that there is such a heavy business interest in the provision of health care means that commercial factors influence the type and quality of treatment that is provided.

The relationship between doctors and drug companies illustrates this point vividly. So, for example, when a doctor wants to choose a drug for a particular patient he will make his decision after referring to information supplied to him by the manufacturers of the available product. Even if he uses apparently independent journals to help him make his drug selection he still cannot be sure that the information he is using is offered without any subjective interest. There are some medical journals which allow drug companies to buy space in which to have their own articles printed. There are many medical journals which are wholly dependent for their very existence on drug company advertising. The result is that when a doctor prescribes a drug he will probably do so largely via information supplied by the drug manufacturer.

Another important consequence of this close relationship between doctors and the drug industry is that forms of therapy which cannot be packaged, marketed and turned into a profitable product are likely to be ignored, both by the medical journals and by the doctors who obtain their information from those journals. Although there is now a growing amount of independent evidence to show, for example, that individuals with high blood pressure can obtain a permanent reduction in their pressure by learning how to relax, most doctors in practice still believe that drugs are the only answer. Only those doctors prepared to look outside the drug-company sponsored literature and journals for their information are likely to hear about such non-commercial remedies.

Preventative programmes are unimaginative and ineffective

When orthodox medical practitioners do offer their patients anything in the way of preventative medicine, they do so without imagination and without any real understanding of what patients need and what will be effective. Too often, for example, doctors run health-education campaigns which are discouragingly negative and which depend upon the patient being told not to do this and not to do that. This mass of negative advice is often confusing and contradictory - and it is usually ignored.

The one type of preventative-medicine technique which doctors seem to favour is the one which includes a medical check-up or a `screening'. Although it would perhaps be unduly cynical to suggest that doctors favour check-ups because they can charge a fee for them, it is nevertheless true that they fit in very well with the traditional type of doctor-patient relationship, in which the patient provides his body and the doctor provides all the expertise, makes all the decisions and takes all the responsibility.

Ironically, the evidence suggests that although check-ups are popular they are of dubious value. In an officially financed British study it was found that there was no significant difference in the health of individuals who had been regularly screened for seven years and those who had not. A study of 7,000 patients showed that people who had had health checks were no more or less likely to lose time from work, to need admission to hospital, to have to visit their family doctor or to die any sooner than patients who had not had them.

In Canada a Task Force on the Periodic Health Examination studied the question for three years before coming to the conclusion that the annual check-up should be abandoned. The conclusion of this official survey was that annual check-ups are not only inefficient but that they are at times potentially harmful.

This last suggestion may seem surprising, but there is good sense in it. By definition annual health checks can only provide an assessment of an individual's clinical condition at the moment. There can be no guarantee that a man pronounced fit on a Monday will not have developed early signs of a life-threatening disease by Friday. Because he has been declared `fit', however, there is a risk that he may ignore the subsequent warning sign. The truth is that a medical screening examination gives no more idea of health than a random bank statement gives any useful idea about financial status. And just as a random bank statement can give a customer false confidence, so a random health check can give a patient false confidence.

To give specific example, I think it is far more useful to teach a woman how to examine her own breasts for lumps or how to be aware of potential danger signs than it is to suggest that she attends a screening once a year.

I do believe that by persuading patients to have annual health checks doctors are encouraging them to abandon their own responsibilities and to rely too heavily on the medical profession. There is an old Chinese proverb that says: `Give a man a fish and you feed him for a day. Teach him how to fish and you feed him for a lifetime.'

It isn't too difficult to see that proverb in medical terms. I wonder if it is too cynical of me to point out, moreover, that if you teach a man to fish you're not likely to be able to sell him many more fish in the future?

The hazards of interventionist medicine

There is a horrifying amount of evidence to show that hospitals are breeding grounds for infective organisms. Even before doctors knew how infections were transmitted, it was recognised that if you were brave enough to put a foot in a hospital you'd be lucky not to end up with both feet in the grave. You might think that things are different in modern hospitals, but you'd be wrong. Today there is evidence indicating that if you are an in-patient in hospital and you have an infection of any kind, then the odds are that you picked it up in the hospital. If you have a wound infection or a urinary tract infection, it is almost certain that you acquired your infection in the hospital.

There is even evidence that hospital canteens and dining rooms can do damage. Gross malnutrition, energy malnutrition and specific deficiency diseases are far too common. Patients can actually waste away in hospital because they have not been fed properly. Scurvy, beri beri and pellagra have all been found among hospital patients, and you're probably more at risk of getting an infection from hospital food than you are if you eat out in a restaurant.

Hospital investigations and treatments can be dangerous as well. The risks are so great that doctors use such words as `idiopathic', `cryptogenic', `iatrogenic' and `nosocomial' to disguise the truth about how diseases have developed.

Potentially dangerous investigations are still performed when there is little or no chance of the patient benefitting from the experience. Too few doctors ask themselves whether such an investigation is justified. Similarly, too few ask themselves whether a particular form of treatment is justified. Today, something like one in ten hospital beds are occupied by people suffering from the treatment they have received. If a patient has tow sets of symptoms, the chances are that the second set of symptoms was caused by the treatment for the first.

The most telling evidence to support my contention that hospitals and doctors can damage your health is simply this: when patients are denied medical help they often live longer. In 1973 when there was a month long doctors' strike in Israel the mortality rate fell by 40 per cent. In 1976 there were doctors' strikes in Colombia and Los Angeles County. In both places the mortality rate fell appreciably. I know of no evidence that mortality rates have ever risen during or immediately after a doctors' strike.

Modern medicine is less effective than you may think

When asked to provide evidence to show that modern medicinal practices are effective, doctors will sometimes point to the way that morbidity and mortality rates have improved since the middle of the 19th century. It is usually claimed that these changes followed improvements in the worlds of medicine and surgery. In fact, however, a closer study of the statistics will show that the most significant improvements took place well before most of the major medical developments took place. It was social changes and not advances in medical technology that helped to cut mortality rates.

The technological advances of which doctors are so proud have, in contrast, made relatively little difference to sickness and death rates. Indeed, recent figures show that in some of the most developed parts of the world life expectancy is little changed today from a half a century ago.

Patients easily become overdependent

A woman in England was once told by her doctor to stay in bed until he returned. He forgot to go back. She stayed in bed for twenty years.

Recently I heard about a man in his fifties who had spent his life avoiding stresses and strains because he had been told that he had a weak heart. The advice had been given when he was a child. A second examination, half a century after the first, showed that the initial diagnosis had been wrong. The man had lived as an invalid for no good reason.

These two sad anecdotes illustrate vividly how patients put too much faith in what their doctors tell them. There are, around the world, many millions of people who have handed over all responsibility for their health to their physicians. These patients suffer because their overdependence limits their lives in many different ways.

The hazards of drug therapy

Three out of every four patients who go and see a doctor come away either with a prescription or a bottle of pills. The majority of doctors believe that patients will be dissatisfied if they leave the consulting room without some sort of therapy.

Consequently, millions of patients take drugs they don't need. And since modern drugs are often dangerous, this in turn means that patients who should never have been given drugs will suffer unnecessarily. Modern drugs can be lifesaving; but they should be used sparingly and with caution.

Your internal defences can be damaged

Interventionists treat the patient as a battleground, the illness as an enemy or target and the armoury of drugs and other treatment aids as weapons with which to fight the illness. Whether the interventionists offer tablets, herbs or the knife, they will be struggling to oppose the body's own internal responses as well as the outside agent which triggered these responses. Indeed, in many cases they may well be fighting only the body's own internal responses. Very many disorders are nothing more than misapplied internal physiological responses, triggered by unseen external threats or imagined threats. Often the result is a continuing struggle - if the initial discontent remains unidentified, the interventionist will have to oppose a continuing physiological response.

Because they must be powerful if they are successfully to oppose powerful physiological responses inside the body, modern treatment forms are likely to create considerable side-effects. So, for example, if a patient with stress-induced high blood pressure takes a drug to control that blood pressure, the drug will have an effect on the whole circulatory system. The drug must continually oppose normal healthy responses to an outside threat which is being ignored and not treated. There is a cruel irony here: for the physiological response is, of course, logical and, as far as the body is concerned, healthy.

In many cases there is an additional hazard associated with this type of interventionist therapy, in that the outside treatment may well have a significant effect on the body's capacity to deal with other threats. If steroids are used as a therapeutic aid, for example, the body will stop producing its own supply of steroids. As far as the body is concerned, there is no need to maintain resources capable of providing immediate supplies in an emergency if there is an apparently endless supply coming from outside the body. Similarly, if pain relievers are used, then the body's production of its own pain-relieving endorphins will not only be reduced but will also be less efficient.

With the body's internal defences damaged and weakened, the individual will have become even more reliant on interventionists and their treatments.

An overemphasis on treatment

Traditionally, individual doctors earn their living by providing patients with medical care when they are ill. Even in those parts of the world where there is no direct link between illness and money, there is still a very powerful feeling that it is the doctor's role to offer advice only when the patient has symptoms. In countries such as Britain, where doctors are paid by the State, there are still very few practitioners prepared to offer their patients advice on how to stay healthy. The emphasis os on healing. Thus diseases are often allowed to progress before treatment is offered.

Normal - an interventionist's myth?

Many interventionists believe that one of their prime roles is to help restore their patients to normal. Whether the abnormality is a symptom such as a pain, a loss of function, or a sign such as an allegedly `abnormal' laboratory result, the aim of the practitioner will be to get things back to normal.

And that can be difficult. For contrary to popular opinion there is no such thing as a `normal' or `average' human being. Doctors used to think that they could measure the properties and functions of the human body in very precise terms, but it is now widely accepted that the range of so-called `normal' values can be vast. What might be normal for you might be an indication of ill health for me.

An interventionist therapy designed to restore you to `normal' may well do directly the opposite.

Alternative medicine - a real alternative or a variation on a theme?

Disillusioned with the medical care offered by orthodox medical practitioners, growing numbers of people are looking for help and satisfaction among the many different types of alternative medicine which are available today. Anxious to boost the speed at which their businesses are growing, many professionals in the `alternative' sector have implied that their solutions offer great advantages over traditional medicine, that side-effects are non existent, that solutions are more reliable and that risks are much reduced.

There are dangers here for some so-called alternatives are merely variations on the same traditional interventionist theme -and there can be no doubt that side effects do exist but are often overlooked. Alternative medicines may appear to offer new and exciting solutions, but in practice the consumer still has to put himself in the hands of someone else and must exchange his allopathic adviser for an acupuncturist, a hypnotist, a herbalist or whatever. The risks remain and we should all be aware of them.

Alternative remedies offered by professional healers are part of the interventionist process - and not an `alternative' to *Bodypower*. I firmly believe that when conditions do need interventionist therapy then a truly holistic approach (incorporating the most appropriate and most effective allopathic and alternative remedies) is wise. Remember that the REAL alternative form of medical care is *Bodypower*.

Home treatments

Home treatments are merely a very simple form of interventionist medicine. If you have a headache, a skin rash or an attack of diarrhoea and you use a drug you have bought over the pharmacist's counter to help ease them, you will be interfering with your body's own response without necessarily understanding the cause of the symptoms. You'll be interfering, or intervening, in just the same way that an orthodox or alternative practitioner will intervene.

When symptoms are inconvenient or uncomfortable, however, home remedies may offer a useful, albeit temporary, solution. They may enable you to disguise or delay those symptoms. Home remedies may have a part to play even when you have mastered the principle of *Bodypower*. For example, if you develop diarrhoea shortly before you are due to attend an important dinner or catch an aeroplane, it won't be much comfort to know that your diarrhoea is caused by your body's efficient attempts to get rid of invading bacteria. A remedy may help provide temporary - but much needed - relief by opposing your body's actions.

The important thing to remember, nevertheless, is that when you are using a home remedy you are suppressing symptoms which suggest an underlying problem. Home remedies must therefore be mild in action and they should never be used for more than five days at a time.

I suggest that if you want to keep a home medicine chest you stock it with the following treatments. These are all simple, safe items if used with care.

1 A pain reliever, such as soluble aspirin or paracetamol tablets. Aspirin is probably slightly better than paracetamol, since it has a stronger anti-inflammatory action. The correct dosages should be marked on he bottles or packaging. A hot-water bottle is also an excellent pain reliever. When wrapped in a pillowcase or thin towel, it can be held against a painful abdomen, joint or ear. Pain relievers should only be used to supplement *Bodypower* pain-relieving techniques. Remember that pain is merely a symptom. Thus, if you have a painful ankle joint and you relieve the pain with a hot-water bottle, you should still be careful not to put too much pressure on the joint. With the pain gone there is often a temptation to treat the joint as normal, often leading to further damage.

2 An indigestion remedy. You don't need to buy an expensive branded product. There are many suitable preparations on the market, but ordinary aluminium hydroxide mixture or tablets will probably be suitable for most occasional attacks of indigestion. Do remember that indigestion is often caused by stress or poor eating habits.

3 A laxative. If you are constipated, the answer is usually to make some adjustment to your diet. Strong, chemical products simply contradict and struggle to overcome a natural response to poor

eating habits. Bran is one of the simplest and quickest diet additives, but fresh oranges also work well. If neither bran nor oranges are effective and your constipation persists, you should seek an interventionist practitioner for advice.

4 An anti- diarrhoeal mixture. If you suddenly develop an attack of diarrhoea, you have probably eaten something that was infected. Your body is simply trying to get rid of the infection as quickly as possible. The best solution is to eat nothing for 36 hours and to drink plenty of fluids. The diarrhoea will then usually stop automatically. If you must stop the diarrhoea while you attend to an important engagement, kaolin and morphine mixture or tablets are as good as anything you can buy.

5 An inhalant. Catarrh and sinus troubles often develop because an irritant has led to the excessive production of fluids within your sinuses. If the symptoms persist and you want relief, inhale the steam rising from a bowl of hot water. Add a menthol crystal to the water for greater effect.

6 A bottle of calamine lotion will help relieve the discomfort associated with itchy spots and rashes.

Interventionist medicine - conclusions

1 Nine times out of ten your body will be able to deal with problems itself. Interventionist medicine will not improve the speed with which you get better.

2 The best forms of interventionist medicine are the ones which support the body's natural healing processes rather than fight them. If you have lost a lot of blood and you are taken to hospital, the doctors will help your body's defence mechanisms by adding fluids to your blood stream. If you have grazed your knee and you clean the wound with fresh water, you'll be helping nature.

3 None of the alternative forms of medicine offer a direct and plain advantage over orthodox medicine. When alternative remedies are as potent and as powerful as orthodox remedies, they are often as potentially dangerous - particularly if used carelessly or improperly. Some alternative remedies which seem to offer less potent remedies are simply relying on your body's recuperative powers. If you need sophisticated help (diagnostic service or surgical support) you will need orthodox medicine anyway. When you have a condition which needs interventionist therapy then you should aim for a truly holistic approach - using the best of orthodox medicine and the best of alternative medicine.

4 You should be aware of the early warning danger signs so that you can take advantage of interventionist medicine when it is needed.

Bodypower in perspective

The human body has an enormous range of mechanisms designed to help provide you with protection and to accelerate the healing processes. These internal mechanisms are so effective that in at least 90 per cent of all illnesses you will be able to recover perfectly well by yourself - without any form of medical treatment. If you are aware of the existence of these mechanisms, prepared to allow your body to repair itself and if you understand how to take advantage of the systems that exist within the body, you will often be able to survive potentially damaging diseases without any need for interventionist therapy.

I must make it clear that I am not advocating that you ignore your doctor altogether. On some occasions, interventionists can provide an essential, life-saving service. They can offer surgical remedies for problems which are not self-limiting and they can offer nursing care and facilities for the disabled and the weak. They can provide diagnostic services and skills, too.

What I am suggesting is that you should become aware of your body's recuperative powers, you should learn to use those powers and you should learn to recognise when you are likely to need professional help, ensuring when you do so that you retain control of your body, bringing in your doctor as an adviser and technical expert rather than as someone in sole charge.

Bodypower is not a replacement for interventionist medicine, but a system designed to ensure that you get the best of both worlds: benefitting from your body's ability to heal itself but also being prepared to use powerful and potentially hazardous professional, interventionist remedies when your body's capabilities reach their limits.

If you ask a lifeguard to hold your head above water every time you go swimming, you will never learn true independence in the water. Learning to use *Bodypower* is like learning to swim. Once you've mastered the idea and gained a little confidence you will soon find yourself enjoying a freedom that you might not otherwise have known. The important point is that - just as the swimmer can call in the lifeguard if he finds himself in trouble - so you can call in the doctor if you need him.

If you have a headache and you visit the doctor, you'll probably get pills. That is what the doctor has been trained to provide. If you learn to use the principles of *Bodypower*, you may well be able to treat your headache yourself. Should you fail, you can still visit the doctor. That's the beauty of Bodypower. You've got everything to gain. And nothing to lose.

PART 3: THE BASIC PRINCIPLES OF BODYPOWER

You will, by now, be fully aware that your body has powerful inner healing mechanisms - and that interventionist techniques usually favoured by health advisers of all kinds often oppose those in-built mechanisms. In this section I'm going to tell you how you can get the best out of your body's own resources.

You must understand that your body isn't designed for modern living

Stone Age man was well equipped to cope with life. He was provided with automatic mechanisms which enabled him to keep his internal body environment stable and which helped to ensure that he ate the right foods at the right time and in the right quantities. He was fitted with automatic mechanisms which allowed his body to prepare itself for a whole host of different dangers.

Today we all live in a world for which we are sadly ill suited. And there are a number of reasons why our bodies are no longer well designed for our environment.

Here are some of them:

1 The world in which we live has changed so comprehensively that we can no longer deal with our problems simply by using our bodies' physical powers. We have to catch buses to the shops, wait in queues to be served and earn money to buy our food. We can no longer escape our predators by running away either. They come after us with lawyers, telephone calls and mail!

2 The human body is designed for immediate action, but many of today's problems cannot be dealt with so quickly. If one of your ancestors was being chased by a sabre-toothed tiger, he would either survive or die in a matter of minutes. If you yourself are unemployed, your problem may persist for months or even years, and your body's responses will continue for the same period. Your body cannot differentiate between short-term problems and long-term problems. The society in which we live has changed very rapidly, but the human body takes thousands of years to evolve. It will be far into the future before man's automatic defence mechanisms have been able to adapt to the demands of twentieth-century life.

3 Many of the problems which cause the greatest amount of pressure are outside our control. If you live in a city, for example, you will be dependent on many people you'll never meet. You'll rely on others to provide you with heat and light and transport. If you had to provide your own facilities, you might be able to do something about them in times of crisis; but in a modern complex society we are all somewhat impotent.

4 Many of the machines and pieces of equipment which were originally designed to work on our behalf are now so complicated and sophisticated that they are the principals and we, the human beings, are the assistants. Consequently, our work may be boring, unsatisfying and sometimes degrading. Workers may find it necessary to go on strike in order to establish

their sense of personal identity; and when they do, they create additional problems for others.

5 Life is changing at an unprecedented rate. Children have to accept that many of the things they are learning at school will be out of date by the time they leave. In the world of science, a graduate may be full of worthless knowledge by the time he collects his graduation papers. Economic changes, social changes and political changes occur at a pace that most of us find heady and unnerving.

6 Our social structure has become so complicated and our capacity for thought and imagination so well developed that we can see problems even where there aren't any. Our body's powers can easily be misapplied if our brains interpret social problems as physical threats. We are manipulated by political, religious and commercial leaders. And we manipulate one another. When these manipulations make us feel frustrated, incompetent or guilty, they lead directly to stress. And that stress leads to a physiological reaction which will invariably be inappropriate.

All-in-all the character of everyday existence has altered so rapidly in the last few decades that the survival mechanisms which were of inestimable value a few hundred or thousand years ago are today more of a handicap than a help. The human body has not had time to adapt to the demands of the new world and nor has it had time to learn to differentiate between situations which are genuinely threatening and which require a physical response and situations which are simply worrying and for which a physical response would probably be harmful.

Appreciate how your body's responses to pressure can produce illness

Many of the diseases which cause trouble today are produced by the fact that the human body has misinterpreted pressures and has overreacted. In many instances heart disease, ulcers, or high blood pressure develop because powerful physiological responses have been brought into action.

It is important to realise, however, that your body's automatic defence mechanisms shouldn't be blamed for the problems that develop. Your body has merely been responding in the way that it was designed to respond. It is the changes in the types of environmental pressure to which you are exposed and the changes in the demands which are implicit in the society in which you live, that have made your physiological responses inappropriate.

If you develop symptoms which are a result of your body's defence mechanisms overreacting, you should endeavour to change your exposure to stress or to change your mental response to it. Treating symptoms produced by your body's defences without treating the basic problems can at best, offer only a temporary solution.

Learn how you respond to pressure by being aware of your personality

Put under the same sort of pressure one man will develop a peptic ulcer while another will acquire an elevated blood pressure. Faced with almost identical problems one woman will acquire asthma, another will develop a skin condition.

It is now known that the reason for these variations lies within the individual personalities of the patients concerned. The personality of an individual will have a significant effect on the type of disorder from which he will be most likely to suffer.

The importance of this particular relationship lies in the fact that by understanding a little about your own personality you will be able to tell what sort of problems you are most likely to face. And by knowing what sort of problems you have to face, you can be better aware of the early warning signs. If you've ever built a sandcastle on the beach and then struggled to find the weak spots and spot the cracks in the walls as they appear, you'll know that an understanding of your own psychological weak points will be invaluable when it comes to fighting off stresses and strains and the signs and symptoms of the illness which ensues.

I don't suggest that the notes which follow are exhaustive. But the pen portraits I've drawn are based on solid clinical work which has been done around the world.

THE ASTHMA PERSONALITY

Asthma sufferers often have domineering mothers and rather ineffectual fathers. Their mothers are frequently overprotective and usually rather indulgent. It is more common for children without brothers or sisters to start the wheezing which is an early sign of asthma, perhaps because only children are more likely to be susceptible to the pressures exerted by this type of parental combination. The tendency is for helpless, dependent and fatalistic asthma sufferers to believe that it is wrong to express their emotions. They don't allow themselves to show their anger, their fears, their tears or their joy. They are usually lonely, somewhat oversensitive souls.

THE ULCER PERSONALITY

People susceptible to ulcers tend to be very dependent on their mothers. They usually need a lot of love. They're sometimes not quite sure whether they want to remain dependent or become independent. They tend to be ambitious and hard-working.

THE DEPRESSIVE PERSONALITY

Patients who suffer from depression tend to feel helpless, inadequate and ineffectual. They usually think little of themselves, are often intolerant and overconscientious and don't usually have much of a sense of humour. Because of their rigid approach to life, they find it especially difficult to adapt to fresh circumstances and new pressures. They're particularly likely to become ill at times of crisis.

THE HEART ATTACK PERSONALITY

If you are aggressive, impatient, intensely competitive and anxious to succeed, you may end up in a coronary care unit attached to an electrocardiograph.

Way back in 1910 William Osler wrote in The Lancet that it is the ambitious, hard-working man who is most likely to have heart pain. In 1945 a doctor concluded that people who have heart attacks do so because they are forever competing with their fathers. Since then, growing numbers of researchers have managed to amplify both these statements. In her book Biotypes Jean Arehart-Treichel recounts that in the early 1950s an upholsterer repairing chairs in a reception room shared by two doctors noticed that only the front edges of the chairs were worn - as though the patients who had been sitting there had been literally `on edge'. The two doctors were called Rosenman and Friedman and they spent a large part of the next two decades trying to find out more about the type of patient likely to have heart attacks.

They discovered that the people who were getting heart attacks were usually male and commonly under great pressure. They managed to show that these men usually had a strong drive to compete and to achieve. The heart attack patient works long hours, sets out to succeed, finds it difficult to sit still, is unable to relax and is a perfectionist. No matter how successful he is, he will rarely be able to fulfil his ambitions.

And, of course, it's not how successful you are that determines your sense of satisfaction - but how successful you think you are.

THE ECZEMA PERSONALITY

Individuals who suffer from chronic skin conditions tend to be rather sensitive. Like asthma sufferers, they tend to repress their emotions. When they get angry they keep it to themselves and when they want to cry they bottle up their emotions. These are common symptoms among people who tend to be allergy victims.

THE ARTHRITIS PERSONALITY

Arthritis sufferers tend to be rather timid, shy and dissatisfied with their own work. They are hard taskmasters. They often come from unhappy homes and there is frequently a history of one parent in particular being hard, domineering and even cruel.

Although they frequently build up a false front, arthritis sufferers are often obsessed with a sense of their own inferiority. They like to conform and they feel helpless in some ways. Arthritis sufferers also have difficulty in expressing their feelings.

THE COLITIS PERSONALITY

The sort of person most likely to develop colitis will be shy, dependent, passive and anxious to please. He'll be indecisive, rather immature and always extremely anxious to avoid conflicts with others. He'll be bright, touchy and emotionally rather labile - bursting into tears quite easily.

THE CANCER PERSONALITY

Back in the 2nd century Galen noticed that women who were depressed were far more likely to develop cancer than women who were happy. In recent years we've acquired considerable evidence to support that early observation. Today it is known that people who are cancer-prone tend to try too hard to please the world. When they fail, as they inevitably must, they get cancer.

Cancer sufferers often have unhappy childhoods and frequently grow up suffering from a lack of love, a sense of loneliness and a feeling that they have been deserted by those closest to them. Cancer victims tend to give more than they take; they tend to repress their own desires and their own emotional feelings. Unselfishly, they do their best to please those around them. When anything goes wrong with the world they've created for themselves, they develop cancer.

Incidentally, it has in the past been suggested that women who breastfeed are less likely to get cancer of the breast because of some aspect of the feeding process. Could it be, I wonder, that the sort of generous, open, loving women who choose to breastfeed are not the sort of women who are particularly likely to develop cancer anyway?

THE MIGRAINE PERSONALITY

Migraine victims are driven by guilt. They feel that they must always strive to do what is right and to satisfy their own over-demanding consciences. The average migraine sufferer is a perfectionist, very ambitious, anxious to please and hard-working. He'll be very neat, very orderly, very efficient and he'll invariably respect achievement and success.

These would all be very valuable traits if they weren't taken that little bit too far. The migraine personality can't meet his own high standards. He'll often fly into a rage when things go wrong. And it is that sort of frustration (produced either by his own failure or by some outside force) that leads to the migraine symptoms.

THE HAY FEVER PERSONALITY

Hay fever sufferers often seem to be timid, nervous people who lack confidence and who are rather obsessive. They are particularly badly affected by crises and traumas and their hay fever may get worse when things are going badly for them.

This list is by no means complete. And there will be people who do not fit neatly into these categories. But if you are aware of your own personality, you will be able to look for some of the appropriate early warning signs. Thus, if you are over-demanding and excessively ambitious, you should beware of those chest pains which suggest that you are putting your heart under pressure. If you are convinced that you have an arthritic personality, you would be wise to be very careful if you have any joint pains.

You must create your own philosophy of Bodypower

The *Bodypower* philosophy must be a very personal thing. I cannot give you a fixed set of rules and tell you to go away and follow them. Your body is unique. So are the stresses and strains in your life. And so are the powers within you.

To use *Bodypower* you must be prepared to create your own *Bodypower* campaign, to employ your skills and abilities as best you can, to learn to listen to your body and to learn to take advantage of your own strengths.

On the pages which follow I have detailed the ways in which you can best achieve these objectives.

Learn to listen to your body

If you will learn to listen to it, your body will be able to tell you a great deal. Many minor symptoms which we regard as a nuisance and which we hurry to treat are early signs that something is wrong. Other signs are simply ignored because we are not aware of their importance or because we aren't aware even of their existence.

For example:

1 If you are lifting or moving something and you feel a twinge of pain, consider that a warning. If you persist you're probably going to end up with a strained muscle or a damaged joint. If you're digging in the garden and your back begins to ache, that's an early sign. If you're lifting heavy boxes and your back begins to hurt, treat that as a warning. Most episodes of pain should be regarded as early warning signs - the longer you ignore a pain, the more likely you are to end up with a serious problem.

2 Vomiting and diarrhoea may be extremely inconvenient, but they are important defence mechanisms employed by your body for specific purposes. If you develop either of these symptoms without any other signs, the chances are that you have acquired some form of gastro-intestinal infection. Remember that any treatment you choose to employ to control your symptoms may also ensure that the infection stays in your body for longer.

3 The cough reflex is a sophisticated defence system designed to eject unwelcome foreign matter from the respiratory tract. You should help your body, therefore, by spitting out anything that you cough up. If you have a persistent or recurrent cough then you must have a persistent or recurrent infection or irritation in your lungs. Or there must be an irritant of some kind in the air you breathe.

4 If you develop an unusual or unexpected skin rash the chances are high that you have been in contact

with an irritant. The reaction of the skin is a result of the fact that the skin tissues, recognising the irritant as a threat, have produced chemicals designed to counteract it. You can probably ease the resultant rash by using powerful drug therapy to oppose the body's reaction. But it is far more sensible to identify the irritant and avoid it.

5 If you develop cramp in your legs it is usually because your circulation has been impeded. The cramp pains develop because the waste products from the metabolic processes which occur during muscle use have accumulated. The slowing down of the circulation has meant that the blood has not been able to clear the wastes away. The cramp pains tell you to change position. Once you have acted the blood will flow more easily. The waste products can then be washed away, and the pain will disappear.

6 Eat the wrong sort of food or eat too quickly and you'll develop indigestion. Your stomach is telling you that you're doing something wrong. You can solve the problem temporarily by using antacids or by taking tablets. Do that, however, and the pains will probably come back. Te get rid of the symptoms permanently you must listen to your symptoms and take notice.

7 If you are for ever having accidents, it may be that you are constantly under too much pressure. There is a strong correlation between accident proneness and stress.

8 A woman who has irregular menstrual periods may well be worried about something. Girls who are taking examinations often have delayed periods - and so do girls who think they may be pregnant.

9 When a pregnant woman is under stress her baby may suffer. There is a strong correlation between maternal stress and babies born with low birthweights or congenital abnormalities. Pregnant women should be on the look-out for signs of stress.

10 Blood pressure often rises when an individual is under pressure. Taxi drivers, schoolteachers and casualty surgeons are far more likely to develop high blood pressure than accountants, church ministers or farmers. It is perhaps a sad reflection on the way most Western people live that a third of the entire American nation is said to suffer from hypertension, while two of the diseases most commonly associated with high blood pressure, strokes and heart disease, are common among men in their twenties and thirties.

The reason for this is simple. When an individual is under pressure his heart will beat faster in order to ensure that his tissues get a better supply of blood. As far as the heart is concerned, it is doing the tissues a favour. Unfortunately, of course, few modern stresses can be resolved with the aid of a faster heart rate and better oxygenated muscles. The man who is under pressure because he is unemployed, worried about his bank loan or threatened with eviction will not benefit from his body's reaction - but he will be warned.

Your early warning systems

Your body has a whole range of special early warning systems. These are designed to give you advance notice of any problems which seem likely to arise and to ensure that potential damage is kept to a minimum.

For example, if your heart is under too much strain and the small vessels which supply it with blood are not able to pump in fluid at a fast enough rate, you will start to suffer chest pains. These pains, usually known as angina, are not in themselves life-threatening. Nor do they suggest that there is any desperately serious life-threatening disorder present. You are being told that your heart has reached its limits and that if you want to avoid any further damage you must make some adjustments to your way of life. You must either change your eating and exercise habits so that your heart can enjoy a better blood supply or you must reduce its workload.

Angina is probably one of the best-known early warning signs of physical distress, but there are many others. Indigestion, for example, is nothing more than an indication that your stomach is finding it difficult to cope with the quality and quantity of food that you're putting into it. Muscle cramps that come on during exercise are an early sign intended to show you that your muscles are using up oxygen and food faster than fresh supplies are being provided.

Although many of the most obvious early warning signs relate to specific physical illnesses, there are also those which are intended to tell you when your body is run down and when you are in genuine need of a rest. When the problem is a general one, the signs will usually appear as a whole series of apparently trivial ailments. You may suddenly find that you are getting lots of coughs and colds, or that you are suffering from spots and boils.

Just as the body can get tired and may show early signs of physical distress, so the mind can become world weary and may need a break from the daily pressures. For example, you may feel lethargic, off-colour or generally out-of-sorts - all these vague symptoms may suggest that you have been pushing yourself too hard. If you are unusually irritable or impulsive, if your memory begins to fail you, if you can't get to sleep, if you become intolerant of noise, if your ability to concentrate seems to have gone or if your willpower seems to have disappeared, if you find yourself crying, overreacting and unable to deal with trivial tasks, the chances are high that you have been doing too much. Your mind needs a rest.

Many people do recognise that these are all signs of overwork and excess pressure, but find themselves unable to do anything constructive to help themselves because they feel guilty if they stop working. Those of us who refuse to listen to these simple warning signs and to take notice of our bodies when they tell us to take things easy for a while, should perhaps remember that some of the greatest men and women the world has ever known happily cut themselves off from all outside contacts whenever they felt themselves to be under too much pressure. Charles Darwin used to pretend to be physically ill in order to give himself a chance to rest in bed whenever he felt himself to be under too much strain. So did Florence Nightingale, Marcel Proust, Sigmund Freud and many others.

Carried to excess, this type of behaviour may well be described as malingering. Employed with care and thought, it is more accurately described as common sense.

Learn to know your weak points

Most of us have a weak point. When we are under too much stress or too much pressure we develop symptoms of a particular type. Learn to know your weak point - as the symptoms begin to develop, you'll know that you are pushing yourself too hard.

Here are some of the commonest `weak point' signs:

- Headache

- Skin rash

- Indigestion

- Wheezing

- Diarrhoea

- Chest pains

- Palpitations

- Insomnia

- Irritability

All of them show that you are beginning to suffer actual physical damage as a result of the stress to which you have exposed yourself. Your stress threshold has been reached.

Spot your own weak point and act on the warning it provides.

Danger signs

If you are to get the best out of *Bodypower* you must know when to ask for interventionist help. *Bodypower* is not an alternative to orthodox medicine; it is a philosophy designed to enable you to know how to use your body's powers in conjunction with orthodox medical techniques.

You should see a doctor without delay if:

1 You have any unexplained pain which recurs or which is present for more than five days (obviously, severe, uncontrollable pain needs to be investigated without delay).

2 You have any unexplained bleeding - from anywhere.

3 You need to take any home medicine regularly or for five days or more.

4 You notice any persistent change in your body (e.g., a loss or gain in weight, a paralysis of any kind, or the development of any lump or swelling).

5 Any existing lump, wart or other skin blemish changes size or colour, or bleeds.

6 You notice new symptoms when you have already received medical treatment.

7 There are mental symptoms present such as confusion, paranoia, disorientation or severe depression.

Learn to relax your body

Fear, anxiety and stress make your muscle tight. And tight, tense muscles are difficult to control. You'll find it impossible to take advantage of your body's healing powers until you can get rid of the tension. In addition, you'll find it difficult to listen to your body if your tissues are tense.

It is vital that you learn how to relax your body.

This isn't difficult to master. Clench your left fist and you'll be able to see the muscles looking tight and firm. Now let your fist unfold and you'll feel and see the muscles relax. To relax your body all you have to do is stiffen all your muscles and then relax them group by group. That's all there is to it.

To begin with, learn to relax in a quiet place where you won't be disturbed. Lie down if you like.

Eventually you'll be able to relax your muscles wherever you are. At first you'll need to pay attention to what you're doing. Allow a quarter of an hour a day for practice until you've mastered the art of relaxation. In time, you'll be able to relax your body in seconds - at the start you'll need longer.

And do be prepared to practise. You wouldn't expect to be able to play golf in one fifteen-minute session, would you?

Relax your body

1 Clench your left hand as tightly as you can, making a fist with the fingers. Do it well and you will see the knuckles go white. If you now let your fist unfold you will feel the muscles relax. When your hand was clenched the muscles were tensed; unfolded the same muscles are relaxed. This is what you must do with the other muscle groups of your body.

2 Ben your left arm and try to make your left biceps muscle stand out as much as you can. Then relax and let the muscle ease. Let your arm lie loosely by your side and ignore it.

3 Relax your right hand in the same way.

4 Relax your right biceps muscles in the same way.

5 Tighten the muscles in your left foot. Curl your toes. when the foot feels as tense as you can make it, let it relax.

6 Tense the muscles of your left calf. If you reach down you can feel the muscles at the back of your leg firm up as you tense them. Bend your foot back at the ankle to help tighten up the muscles. Then let the muscles relax.

7 Straighten your leg and push your foot away from you. You will feel the muscles on the front of your thigh tighten up; they should be firm right up to the top of your leg.

8 Relax your right foot

9 Relax your right lower leg

10 Relax your right thigh.

11 Lift yourself up by tightening up your buttock muscles. You will be able to lift your body upwards by an inch or so. Then let the muscles fall loose again.

12 Tense and contract your abdominal muscles. Try to pull your abdominal wall as far in as possible. Then let go and allow your waist to reach its maximum circumference.

13 Tighten the muscles of your chest. Take a big deep breath and strain to hold it for as long as possible. Then let it go.

14 Push your shoulders back as far as they will go, then turn them forwards and inwards. Finally, shrug them as high as you can. Keep your head perfectly still and try to touch your ears with your shoulders. It

will probably be impossible but try anyway. Then ley your shoulders relax and ease.

15 Next tighten up the muscles of your back. Try to make yourself as tall as you can. Then let the muscles relax.

16 The muscles of your neck are next. Lift your head forwards and pull at the muscles at the back of your neck. Turn your head first one way and then the other. Push your head backwards with as much force as you can. Then let the muscles of your neck relax. Move it about to make sure that it really is completely loose and easy.

17 Move your eyebrows upwards and then pull them down as far as they will go. Do this several times making sure that you can feel the muscle tightening both when you move the eyebrows up and when you pull them down. Then let them relax.

18 Screw up your eyes as tightly as you can. Pretend that someone is trying to force your eyes open. Keep them shut tight. Then, keeping your eyelids closed, let them relax.

19 Move your lower jaw around. Grit your teeth. Wrinkle your nose. Smile as wide as you can, showing as many teeth as you have got. Now, let all these facial muscles relax.

20 Push your tongue out as far as it will go. Push it firmly against the bottom of your mouth and the top of

your mouth and then let it lie relaxed and easy inside your mouth.

While you do all these simple relaxation exercises take deep, slow, regular breaths. Breathe as slowly as you comfortably can.

Relax your mind

You can counteract the effect of stress and pressure on your body by learning to relax your mind. Under normal circumstances an almost unceasing flood of information and impressions pour into your brain. These pieces of information produce an almost endless number of interpretations and mental assessments. And those mental reactions, in turn, have a noticeable effect on many of the body's physiological processes.

If you can effectively cut the amount of information your mind is receiving, logically you will cut the number of mental responses. Temporarily isolate your brain, and therefore your body, from stimulating inputs and you'll be temporarily isolated from the need for unnecessary physical responses.

Research showing the way that mental relaxation can help the human body has nearly all involved meditation of one form or another. And for several reasons that has discouraged many people from trying to relax their minds.

In the first place, those who teach meditation claim that it is necessary to empty the mind of all inputs and all thoughts in order to benefit from the respite. And that isn't easy. Many people find the prospect of emptying their minds so daunting that they never even try.

Secondly, the religious and semi-religious features which seem to be an essential part of many forms of meditation are frightening and forbidding to a variety of people. They don't want to have to take part in any organised rituals and they would feel self-conscious if they had to sing or chant any magic incantations.

In fact you can enjoy the benefits of mental relaxation without meditating, without joining any religious organisation, without paying any fees, without going into a trance, without adopting any strange habits, without having your hair shaved off, without wearing any odd clothes and without adopting any uncomfortable postures.

All you have to do in order to cut the flood of potentially harmful sensory data which normally streams into your brain is to learn how to daydream.

Or, to be more accurate, to revise your views on daydreaming. For most of us acquire the habit of daydreaming when we are small and are then taught by our teachers and our parents that it is an undesirable habit.

It isn't a bad habit. It is a natural process and a natural method of escape and relaxation which most of us find without training as we grow up in a world full of pressures. Daydreaming is a natural `cut out' process which our brains have created for our own protection. All you have to do is remove socially imposed restrictions, get rid of your guilt and learn to enjoy your daydreaming again.

And if your childhood was so strictly structured that you were never allowed to daydream at all - be assured that nothing could be simpler. Allow yourself to escape into a happy memory. It doesn't matter what the recollection is, as long as it is one which you find pleasantly relaxing without being too stimulating.

The only vital advice I can give you is that you should do everything you can to ensure that the daydream is believable. You must convince yourself (and your body) that the daydream is real. To start with, you'll probably have to lie down somewhere quiet. Later you'll be able to daydream wherever you are - and whatever you're supposed to be doing.

Suppose, for example, that you choose a beach scene from a happy holiday as your first memory. Try to:

*   feel the warmth of the sun on your face

*   allow a gentle breeze to ruffle your hair slightly

*   feel the warm, soft sand underneath you

*   hear the sound of the waves breaking and the cries of the seagulls above

*   smell the salty air and the light perfume of your favourite sun oil.

If you like, you can add someone of whom you are very fond to your daydream. But keep the action quiet and peaceful. Concentrate only on flooding your mind with images of happy memory. Once your mind believes that you are there, your body will be convinced.

The accumulated pressures and stresses that have been battering away at your defences for so long will disappear as your body takes it easy. You can gain just as much from your daydream as you could ever hope to gain from a genuine holiday break. Probably more. You can keep the rain, the flies, the deckchair attendants and the boring travelling out of your daydream.

Of course, you don't have to restrict yourself to one daydream. You can build up a library of your very own, very private daydreams. Store up a whole collection of comforting memories which enable you to escape from the harsh realities of the world. Keep them in some secret room in your head. Then, to daydream effectively, all you have to do will be to wander into your secret room, select a suitable daydream and lie back to enjoy it. The more practice you get, the better skilled you'll become. Before long you'll be able to daydream without anyone being aware of what you're doing.

Daydreaming has an advantage over meditation. Instead of emptying your mind and replacing anxieties and fears with a clinically clean empty space, you will be replacing your fears with loving, comfortable memories which will themselves have a good and positive effect.

When you empty your head of damaging thoughts and fill it with joy and love you don't just halt the damage - you do more. You can build up your inner strength. Negative emotions, such as fear, can do much harm. But positive emotions, such as love and happiness, can contribute greatly to your all-round health.

Let your emotions show

Do you remember when Nikita Kruschev took off his shoe at the United Nations? He was annoyed by something that had been said and revealed his feelings by using his shoe to pound on the conference table. It might not have been the sort of thing a well-trained gentleman would do, but it was probably the right reaction as far as his health was concerned

Far too many of us prefer to hide our emotions. If we feel angry we try to keep our anger hidden deep inside us. If we feel sad we refuse to allow anyone to see our tears. If we feel proud we don't like to let our pride show. We hide our emotions because we have been taught that it is wrong to do otherwise.

And yet nothing could be more damaging. When we feel that we want to express an emotion and we hide that emotion we are denying a very natural process. We're fighting against a normal human response which should be allowed to influence our actions. Our natural reactions are, after all, designed to help us. When we feel sad and can feel the tears welling up in our eyes, our bodies are trying to help us by making it clear to those who are nearest and dearest to us that we need support and comfort. By refusing to allow our tears to flow - and thus refusing to allow our sorrow to show - we are denying ourselves the comfort that our bodies have decided we need.

Take time out

If you have been pushing yourself particularly hard you may find that you suddenly start to feel tired or lethargic. Or maybe you'll start to suffer all sorts of minor symptoms.

Either way, you've been given a hint to take things a little easier. Your body has been pushed to its limits and it wants a respite.

Many people find it difficult to do just that. They feel that they must keep pushing themselves all the time - and they end up suffering from something far more serious. Having ignored the early warning signs of exhaustion, they find themselves suffering from something much worse.

However tough you are, you can't keep punishing yourself indefinitely. Everyone needs a rest from time to time. If, after an especially difficult patch or a tough stretch of work, you feel shattered or exhausted, you mustn't be afraid to take it easy for a while.

Rocking chair therapy

A child who is very upset and troubled will often sit hunched up and rock backwards and forwards very gently. He'll do this naturally, without any teaching or prompting, because the rocking motion helps to relax the body and drain away accumulated tensions. We don't really know how this works, but what seems to happen is that the rhythmic motion aids in counteracting the urgent messages which are being sent from the muscles to the brain. The feedback somehow opposes the messages which originally inspired the tautness and tightness.

This type of simple, rhythmic exercise is an excellent way to ease and relax the whole body, as anyone who has a rocking chair will confirm. And it is no coincidence, of course, that nursing mothers will often rock their babies backwards and forwards when they are crying.

Aggressive exercise

Your body is designed for action. When things go wrong or you are threatened in any way your body will automatically prepare itself for action. Your muscles will tighten, your blood pressure will go up and your whole body will be made ready for battle.

Sometimes, of course, this type of preparation is entirely appropriate. If you are threatened with a physical crisis of any kind, your body's preparations will be what you need. If you're trying to get out of a burning house or you're trying to escape from a mugger, you'll need every ounce of muscle you've got.

Usually, however, those physical preparations will be totally inappropriate. The problem will be an imaginary one and no amount of physical preparation will improve your capacity to cope. Indeed, physical preparations can often be an embarrassment and may cause damage. Your body will be prepared for action that doesn't come and unnecessary and unsuitable changes will have taken place within your muscles, cardiovascular system and elsewhere.

In those circumstances you may well be wise to adapt your behaviour to fit in with your body's preparations. Like a massive tree that isn't too proud to bend a little with the wind, you should perhaps be prepared to adapt. And consider getting rid of your physical energy.

You can do this in all sorts of ways.

I remember reading about an eminent international banker who walked out of a particularly stressful meeting, wandering straight from the meeting into a nearby fair. There he went directly to one of the stalls, bought an armful of wooden balls and proceeded to destroy large quantities of old china!

The Greeks sometimes do much the same, of course. After a hard day's work they spend a pleasant evening smashing plates on a local tavern floor.

Others prefer to get rid of their pent-up excess energy by taking part in energetic, even violent, sports. Hitting a tennis ball or a squash ball and racing around a court can quickly get rid of the accumulated physical preparations which might otherwise have a damaging effect on your body.

It is important to remember not to become anxious about your sporting prowess when you're getting rid of muscle activity in this way. It is far too easy to exchange one form of stress for another by being too determined to win when taking part in a sport theoretically designed to help you relax.

It's all in the mind

You may not think of yourself as having a powerful, `creative' imagination. But you do have an imagination powerful enough to control your physical destiny. Everyone has.

If you believe that you are going to fail at something, the chances are that you will fail.

If you believe that you are ugly, you will live in a world structured by your ugliness.

If you are walking a tightrope and you believe that you are going to fall, you will probably fall.

In all these circumstances reality is irrelevant. The governing factor is what your imagination tells you. And what you believe.

Take walking a tightrope, for example. If your imagination tells you that you are going to fall and you believe it, your body will begin to react as though you are already falling. You'll see yourself toppling and your muscles will automatically make futile and unnecessary attempts to correct your fall. You'll unbalance as you struggle to maintain your balance. You'll fall.

If you imagine that you are inadequate, you will deal with life as though your inadequacy were a fact and not a thought. You will work without confidence and you will inevitably fail to inspire confidence in others. You may push yourself harder to try and cope with your imagined inadequacy; but - however hard you push - you will never succeed because you will be struggling to overcome something that exists only in your mind. You'll never be able to win. You'll push yourself until you develop genuine signs of illness. And then you'll have `proof' that you will never be able to succeed.

Imagination can have a damaging effect on you and your life.

But, it can also have a positive effect.

Indeed, imagination can be used as a positive, constructive force as simply as it can be used negatively. Your imagination can lead to unhappiness, illness and failure, but it can also lead to happiness, health and success.

With the aid of your imagination you can achieve great things.

If you believe that you are going to succeed at something, the chance are that you will succeed.

If you believe that you are good-looking, you will live in a world structured to good looks.

If you are walking a tightrope and you believe that you are going to cross the rope safely, you probably will cross it.

Wherever you are, whatever you are doing, use your imagination positively.

Learn to appreciate the power of positive emotions

Similarly, if you are overwhelmed with negative emotions, you will be far less capable of coping with stress. If you feel sad, you'll be particularly likely to react badly if things go wrong. If you feel nervous or anxious, you'll be far more likely to suffer when you're under pressure.

Just as negative emotions can have an adverse effect on the mind and body, however, so positive emotions can have a useful, constructive effect. There isn't any conclusive evidence in favour of such a theory, but it does seem very likely that you'll be far less likely to suffer from stress, and far less likely to become ill, if you're feeling bright and cheerful.   Children who are deprived of maternal love are more likely not only to become socially aggressive but also to spend much of their time in later years suffering from ill-health. Love doesn't just make the world go round; it also helps to make it go round more smoothly.

There isn't much indisputable clinical evidence to show that laughter does you good either, but the experiences of Norman Cousins, which are described so vividly in his marvellous book Anatomy of an Illness, strongly suggest that there may well be a relationship between laughter and good health. Cousins, assured by his doctors that there was no cure for an inflammatory disease which threatened to leave him crippled and incapable, left his dreary hospital room, moved into a hotel and spent his days reading witty books and watching funny films.

Not only did he make a remarkable recovery and insist that he obtained genuine relief from pain by laughing, but he - with his doctors - also managed also managed to produce solid laboratory evidence to show that his laughter had a useful, positive effect on his physical condition. There is still some confusion about why this should be, but it seems that laughter may help by improving respiration, by lowering blood pressure and possibly also by increasing the supply of specific types of endorphin in the blood. Certainly it seems more than possible that laughter isn't merely a pleasant experience, but is also a positive, natural phenomenon which helps ensure that the body benefits from pleasant experiences. The researchers are still working in this field, but they have already shown that laughing gas makes us laugh because it stimulates the production of a special endorphin.

Perhaps laughter is the best medicine after all. And if laughter can help, what about hope, confidence, delight and all other pleasures?

Whatever the physiological explanations may be, the implications are far-reaching. A carefree, positive approach

to life may bring much more than passing joy.

The advantages of staying active

One of the saddest sights I know is to see someone retiring, accepting his gold watch and inscribed scroll, and going home to television set, golf clubs and potting shed.

There is now an overwhelming amount of evidence to show that retirement is dangerous to health! If you give up your daily responsibilities, you stand a greater than average chance of becoming mentally or physically ill. You will be more prone to depression, and more prone to stomach, heart and chest troubles, too.

Not that this is surprising when you stop to think about it. After all, when you retire, you may be left with no real purpose to your life. You don't have to get up and go anywhere. You don't have to do anything. You have no responsibilities, no duties and no authority. You are living outside the only society that you know.

And your body will reflect this by failing to function properly. Just as too many demands cause damage, so too few demands can cause damage. You can ruin a car by pushing it too hard, but you can also ruin it by leaving it in the garage for far too long. When there are no demands, the muscles atrophy, the heart slows down and the joints begin to creak and groan. Small problems are allowed to persist because they do not threaten any vital activity. The body's defence mechanisms also begin to slow down.

Consequently, if you then have to face a crisis, you will be ill equipped to cope. Once retired and settled into a lazy rut, you will find that your ability to defeat pressure through your body's powers will be diminished.

After all, if your leg muscles aren't fit and you try running a mile, you'll soon have to stop. The other organs of your body, some of which you cannot see, are affected in exactly the same way when they are allowed slowly to atrophy. If your heart is never put under any sort of pressure, you're more likely to have a heart attack if anything goes wrong. If your lungs aren't used to the full, you're more likely to get chest troubles. And so on.

The secret of a long, healthy life is to try to keep active. By and large, the more you use your mind and body the fitter they will stay.

PART 4:BODYPOWER IN PRACTICE

So much for the general principles of *Bodypower*. In this final section I want to give some specific examples of how *Bodypower* works in practice.

You can use <u>Bodypower</u> to help improve your shape and maintain your health

The fat of the land

People get fat for many different reasons. Some people eat because they are depressed. Others eat too much because they are anxious. Babies who are bottle-fed seem more likely to put on too much weight than babies who are breast-fed. Fat babies often grow into fat children who often grow into fat adults. Obesity seems to run in families, too, although whether it does so because of inherited factors or simply because the family members all sit down and overeat together is a difficult question to answer.

Despite this confusion, we know one thing for certain. Most overweight people need not have got fat if they had listened to their bodies telling them what to eat and when to eat it.

Your appetite control centre, which I have already described and which is directly controlled by the amount of sugar circulating in the blood, is designed to ensure that you eat just what your body needs, exactly when your body needs it. Unfortunately, of course, most of us ignore our appetite control centre completely and adjust our eating habits to fit in with the behavioural patterns imposed on us by the society in which we live.

Our eating habits are usually established when we are children. Inevitably, therefore, it is our mothers who usually set the pattern. If you think back to when you were small, you'll probably remember that you were always encouraged to eat at organised meal times. Your mother doubtless got upset if you didn't want anything to eat and doubtless got even more upset if you didn't clear your plate every time you sat down at the table.

Indeed, if you were bottle-fed your `training' probably started before you could sit down to the table. One reason why bottle-fed babies tend to get fatter than their breast-fed counterparts is that, while it is impossible to see how much has been taken from the breast, it is all to easy to see just how much is left in the bottle! Anxious mothers tend to encourage their babies to empty the bottle even when their babies don't seem hungry.

These distorted behavioural patterns all help to ensure that your appetite control centre is consistently overruled. Your eating habits will eventually be controlled not by your body's genuine need for food but by a totally artificial conception of its requirements. You can be trained to eat badly and unwisely as easily and efficiently as Pavlov's dogs were trained to salivate at the sound of a bell. By the time most of us reach adulthood we're accustomed to eating according to the clock on the wall rather than the clock in our brains. We eat when our parents taught us to eat or when it seems that we ought to eat. We eat what the advertising copywriters tell us we should be eating and we eat it when those around us think we should eat it.

That's the bad news.

The good news is that these damaging eating habits can be reversed as simply as they can be established. By learning to listen for your body's internal signs of hunger, by abandoning habits which overrule your appetite control centre and by eating when you need to eat, you'll find it possible to lose weight or to maintain a steady weight without any external aid or support.

Try this regime:

1 Only eat when you are hungry. Most people eat at pre-ordained times which may or may not bear any relationship to their need for food. It may sound disruptive to suggest that you abandon fixed meal times and in a large family it can certainly cause some confusion. But the disruption will probably be far less severe than you might have imagined. Besides, if you are trying to lose weight, you must not break this rule. Every time you put anything in your mouth (that you intend to eat) you must ask yourself whether you need it; whether you are hungry.

2 Concentrate on what you are doing when you are eating. If you chat, read a magazine, stare at the newspaper, watch television or do the crossword while you're eating, the chances are that you'll miss the signs from your appetite control centre. You have to concentrate on your eating if you are to be aware of the messages telling you that you are full.

3 Don't be afraid to leave on your plate when you are full. It's a waste to throw food away, but isn't the dustbin a more suitable receptacle for waste than your stomach? Many people feel so guilty if they see food being wasted that they eat others' leftovers. This is eating lunacy.

4 Get in to the habit of serving small portions. That way you'll be less inclined to eat too much. And you'll be less likely to have to face the problem of plucking up courage to throw food away. If you consistently find that there is too much food on your plate, try putting less on it to start with. The aim is to stop eating as soon as you're full.

5 Try to build up an awareness of your body's needs. If you eat something very salty, you'll feel thirsty afterwards because your body will try to balance the high salt intake with a higher fluid intake. If you listen to your body when you're hungry, you'll find that it is telling you what you need. Those strange fancies that pregnant women get are often very sensible! If you feel like eating something sweet, eat something sweet. If you feel like an orange, eat an orange - your body probably thinks that you are short of something that an orange can provide.

6 Most of us eat fairly large meals at fairly infrequent intervals because that is the way our society encourages us to eat. This doesn't help your appetite control centre at all. If you eat a meal and then don't eat for several hours, your body will react accordingly. It will expect to receive supplies irregularly. Consequently, it will encourage you to eat as much as possible when you are eating; and it will store what isn't needed. The food is, of course, stored as fat. If you eat smaller meals, but more frequently, the food you take in will be burned up straight away. None of it will be stored. And you'll take in just what your body needs. Eat small meals and eat often!

7 Don't use food as a crutch. If you eat because you are sad or happy or in or out of love, your appetite control centre will become confused. Only eat when you are genuinely hungry.

8 Don't use food as a weapon. Don't force children to eat foods they don't like. Don't deprive them of food if they are naughty. Don't link food and punishment or

food and reward. This sort of behaviour disrupts the appetite control mechanism.

9 Don't think it rude to leave food on the side of your plate when you are out dining. And don't feel bad about turning down courses. Be a gourmet by all means - but not a gourmand!

10 be patient while you are re-educating your body to listen to the dictates of your appetite control centre. If you've been ignoring it for years, it will take a little while for you to learn to listen to it again.

For matchstick men and women

Most people who have a weight problem worry because they are too fat. That isn't always the case. A number of men and women complain that whatever they eat they can't put weight on. Being grossly underweight can be just as embarrassing as being overweight.

Sometimes the problem is caused by a hormonal disorder. The man or woman with an overactive thyroid will burn up food so quickly that he or she will remain skinny however much food is eaten. Often, however, there is no cause that can be treated.

When there isn't a medical reason behind an individual's failure to put on weight, the solution to the problem usually involves a deliberate attempt to overrule the appetite control centre. Unlike the overweight person, the skinny individual will usually eat within very strictly defined limits. An efficient control centre will ensure that he stops eating just before he gets full.

To defeat the body's own appetite control centre, it is necessary to take up some of the bad habits that slimmers usually need to avoid! So, for example:

1 If you think you're too thin and you want to get fatter, trick your body by eating when you're doing something else. That way your appetite control centre won't be able to switch off your desire to eat quite so easily.

2 Gobble up your food faster than usual. When you eat slowly you know when you're full. If you push your food in quickly you'll overfill your stomach before it can pass the message on to your brain.

3 Eat late at night when your body doesn't need much food. A midnight feast is probably the best way of putting on weight.

4 Use a bigger plate than usual, eat bigger meals than you normally manage and don't miss fixed meal times. All these tricks help ensure that your body's appetite control centre is ignored.

More of a good thing

According to clinical research published in very reputable journals, women can use *Bodypower* to help improve the shape and size of their breasts.

One of the most startling and comprehensive research projects on this subject was undertaken by Dr Richard D Willard of the Institute of Behavioural and Mind Sciences in Indiana, who asked 22 female volunteers, ranging in age from 19 to 54, to use self-hypnosis and visual imagery in an attempt to enlarge their breasts. At the start of the study, which was eventually described in full in the American Journal of Clinical Hypnosis, five individual breast measurements were taken for each woman - circumference, height, width and other measurements were recorded by a doctor who was not involved in the experiments. The volunteers then attended Dr Willard's clinic once a week for six weeks and once every two weeks for an additional six weeks.

At the first session the women were taught how to relax their muscles by using the same sort of technique as the one I have already described in this book. Subsequently, they were asked to do this and then to imagine that they had a wet, warm towel draped over their breasts. They were asked to imagine that the towel was making their breasts feel warm, or - if they found this difficult - to imagine that a heat lamp was shining directly onto their breasts.

Once the women were satisfied that their breasts were getting warmer, they were asked to develop an awareness of a pulsation within their breast tissue. It was suggested to them that they should become conscious of their heartbeats and feel each new beat pushing blood into their breasts. They were told to practise this exercise every day at home.

At the end of the 12-week experiment, 28 per cent of the women had achieved the growth in breast size that they wanted, 85 per cent had confirmed that a significant increase in their breast size had been achieved and 46 per cent had reported that they had had to buy bigger bras. The average increase in breast circumference was 1.37 inches; in breast height, 0.67 inches; and in breast width, 1.01 inches. Most women reported that by the end of the experiment they could feel warm blood flowing into their breasts simply by thinking about their breasts.

There were other advantages, too! Those women who had - at the start of the experiment - complained of having breasts of unequal size, reported that their breasts had become equal in size. All the women reported that their breasts were now firmer. And some 63 per cent of the women, who had complained of having pendulous breasts when the experiment had started, reported that the fullness and the contours of their breasts had returned. Incidentally, to make sure that the extra breast size hadn't just been achieved by an increase in weight, the women were also weighed at the start of the experiment. At the end of the 12-week period 42 per cent of the women had actually had a weight loss of greater than 4 pounds, but had all nevertheless noticed an improvement in their breast size.

When he studied the changes Dr Willard found that there was no correlation between the increase in size and the size of the breasts at the start of the experiment. He did, however, find that there was a correlation between the ease with which the women were able to visualise blood flowing into their breasts and the increase in size which they obtained. The only two women who subjectively felt that their breasts had not increased in size (but who did, in fact, have a measurable increase in bosom dimensions) had both had difficulty in feeling the effect of the warmth on their breasts.

In another, similar experiment Allan R. Staib and D. R. Logan of the University of Houston encouraged three women under hypnosis to imagine themselves going back in time to when they were ten or twelve years old. The women were told to imagine that they could feel their breasts pushing outwards and that they could then feel the skin getting tighter as the tissues grew. Then they were asked to imagine themselves standing nude in front of the bathroom mirror some two or three years after the completion of the experiment. They were told to notice that in the intervening time their breasts had become larger.

Staib and Logan managed to show that their volunteers also enjoyed an appreciable improvement in breast size. Moreover, they also revealed that even after three months the greater part of the gain remained.

It is not easy to explain these startling results, but it seems likely that the results obtained by Staib and Logan were, like those obtained by Willard, produced by an increase in the amount of blood flowing through the breasts. Masters and Johnson had indicated in 1966 that the swelling of the female breasts during sexual arousal is produced by an increase in the amount of blood in the tissue.

Biofeedback practitioners have proved many times that the general circulatory system can be controlled voluntarily and these specific research projects provide analogous evidence. But the breast-enlarging programmes do, in addition, show that the increase in circulation may be followed by a consequent tissue growth. And that is most remarkable, for it suggests that there may well be other, even more startling uses for this particular type of self-hypnosis.

Keep young and beautiful

We inherit our basic physical characteristics and all our physical features from our parents. Your body build, for example, is inherited. If you're now too tall, too short, too muscular or too weedy, you only have your parents to blame. And, I would have to add, their parents. And their parents' parents. And their parents' parents' parents. Your most salient physical features are inherited from your parents too. If you have a huge nose, you'll almost certainly find that - even if your parents don't have oversize noses - there is someone up there in your family tree who is equipped with an oversize piece of olfactory equipment.

Sometimes basic characteristics miss a generation or two, with the result that blond parents may suddenly produce a raven-haired child. Occasionally, basic characteristics rarely miss a generation at all. Any Hapsburg mother who produced a child without the famous harelip would probably have found herself being fitted for a new and improved chastity belt. In any event, somewhere in your past there will have been ancestors possessing the features you now possess.

By the time you've reached your mid-twenties you'll be beginning to put your personal stamp on the characteristics you've inherited. Whatever sort of body you were born with, the sort of body you end up with will depend more on the way you have lived than on purely inherited characteristics.

Like any piece of machinery the human body shows signs of ageing according to the way it is treated. Look after your body with care and thought and it will serve you well. If, on the other hand, you treat your body without respect, it will age rapidly. Whatever physical characteristics you inherited, your life style will have a powerful effect on the ageing process.

Clearly, therefore, it is important to know just how to look after your body properly. If you are aware of, and able to take advantage of, your body's natural physiological mechanisms, you will be far better equipped to deal with the numerous pressures which can accelerate the ageing process. If you want to keep young and beautiful, you need to know how to oppose those threats likely to be a problem.

The following list is intended to offer you advice on how best to defy old age.

1 Wrinkles are commonly considered to be inevitable in old age. To a very limited extent that may be true. As we age, our skin does lose some of its elasticity, appearing stretched and loose as a result. At the same time the skin's glands produce less oil and the surface cells become gradually drier. Together these two changes result in the skin becoming wrinkled - in much the same way that a dried-out river bed will gradually become cracked and wrinkled too.

There isn't much you can do to prevent your skin losing its natural elasticity, I'm afraid, but you can help prevent it becoming dry. If you regularly use a moisturising cream to replace the missing natural oils, you will keep the tissues just underneath the surface layer of skin plump and full. You'll be far less likely to develop any wrinkles. Moisturising creams do not add water to the skin, as some experts occasionally suggest, but they do help your body preserve moisture that is already there.

You should also keep out of the sun as much as possible - unless you're using an effective sunscreen agent. Too much sunshine will dry and damage your skin and will increase the rate at which wrinkles develop. A sunscreen cream, applied regularly and liberally, will protect the tissues from the potentially damaging short-wavelength ultraviolet rays while letting through the longer wavelength ultraviolet rays which produce tanning of the skin.

2 It is widely assumed that we are all bound to put on weight as we get older. This just isn't true. Unless your family is blighted with some rare metabolic disorder, your overall size in twenty years time will be more a reflection of your eating habits than any inherited characteristic. Eat with sense, discretion and caution and remember that as you get older and take less exercise so you need fewer calories. You will then stay slim and trim into your retirement years.

3 Joint and muscle disorders, such as the various types of rheumatism and arthritis, are often thought of as diseases of old age. It is true that as they get older joints become worn and muscles become less efficient. It is, however, also true that the disorders which fall into this general category are far more likely to develop when joints and muscles are used irregularly and carelessly than when they are used regularly and wisely. Gentle exercise, carried out to a routine, will help keep muscles supple and joints mobile.

You can also help to minimise your susceptibility to such disorders by resting when you have any pain or deformity affecting a joint and by keeping your weight under control. If you are carrying excess weight your bones and muscles will be under unnecessary extra strain.

4 After their size and their skin the thing most women seem to worry about as they grow older is their shape. Men are often accused of being obsessed with women's breasts and that may well be true, but it is also a fact that women notice the contours of their

chests. I'd like a week's holiday in the South of France for every women I know who worries that one day her pert, well-shaped breasts will end up looking like sacks of rice pudding!

There is no mystery about the changes which affect the female breasts as they age. Breasts, like apples, respond to the urgings of gravity and any woman who is particularly well endowed will sag sooner rather than later. Her less well-endowed sister may not notice any comparable change for some years.

There is no simple, magic solution to the problem of `breast droop', but any woman who wants to delay the onset of the `droop' can do so by wearing a well-supporting bra and by keeping the muscles of her chest wall adequately exercised. A good bra will enable the shoulders to take some of the weight and strain of the breast tissue, while strong chest muscles will be far better able to counteract the effects of gravity.

5 Thinning hair is a problem which worries many older men and women. Baldness in men is, of course, very often inherited. There is nothing that can be done about this type of hair loss. When the loss of hair is not genetically controlled it is frequently the result of carelessness with chemicals of one sort or another; preventative measures can, therefore, be taken.

Hair can be damaged by bleaching, tinting, stripping, straightening or perming. None of these operations should be done very often and as a general rule no more than one should be done within the same seven-day period.

Sun, heat, salt water and chlorinated water may also damage hair. You should wear a sun hat with a broad rim when sunbathing; you should avoid using rollers that are too hot, and you should rinse your hair thoroughly after bathing.

Finally, you should be aware that mechanical damage can result in hair loss. Don't brush or comb your hair too much and don't use too hard a brush or comb. The bristles shouldn't be too sharp or too close together, either. Your hair is particularly likely to be damaged by fierce brushing when it is wet.

6 Older women tend to complain that their hands and fingernails are ugly and badly marked. Human hands and nails are not prepared for frequent immersion in strong chemical solutions. Detergents and bleaches can damage both the skin of the hands and the nails themselves. To avoid problems of this type you should ensure that your hands are well rinsed, dried carefully and covered with a moisturising cream every time they have been dipped in water. The cream will replace the natural oils which have been lost.

7 Decayed or missing teeth are common signs of old age. Dental decay is, indeed, one of the commonest diseases in the Western world and dentists remove tons of teeth every year. This level of decay is not

only responsible for much distress and embarrassment, but also causes poor eating habits. People with missing teeth and bleeding gums find chewing painful, if not impossible.

It is now well established that dietary habits are largely responsible for this epidemic of dental decay. It was in the seventeenth century that people in Britain first began to eat sugar in relatively large quantities and it was then that they first began to suffer from rotting teeth. Medical historians and statisticians have traced and related the increase in dental decay to the increase in the consumption of sugar. More recently, it has been shown that tooth decay among the Eskimos has risen as they have adopted the Western junk diet, with its heavy sugar component.

Clearly, one simple way to reduce the rate of dental decay is to reduce the consumption of sugar-rich foods. Since the worst foods are those which are sipped and sucked, so bathing the teeth in a destructive solution, it is sweets and sugar-rich drinks which are best avoided. It has been estimated that most of us eat approximately two pounds of sugar a week; cutting back should be easy.

There are foods which help maintain the teeth in good condition. Sugar-free foods that need a good deal of chewing help to clean the teeth in a purely mechanical fashion and, by aiding the production of large quantities of saliva, aid in keeping the teeth clean. Obviously, it also helps to develop good tooth-cleaning habits.

8 Many of us treat our bodies with far too little thought. A recent report from America's National Institute for Medicine stated that it is our lifestyle which is killing most of us. The report points out that three-quarters of Americans die from heart diseases, strokes, cancer and accidents or violence. In all those disorders, behaviour, or life style, plays an important part. Cigarette smoking, excessive drinking, reckless driving and poor eating habits are all listed as factors contributing to death or poor health.

These bad habits commonly cause problems when they get out of control. The message is: If you must sin, do so in moderation.

9 I've lost count of the number of people I've known who have led busy, healthy lives, then retired, deteriorated and died soon afterwards. The human body is designed for action and activity. Long before you retire you should make plans which will ensure that you will keep your mind and your body fully occupied.

10 As we get older, our body's defences become weaker and less efficient. Catch a minor infection as a young man and your body will survive with little difficulty. Catch an infection of similar severity half a century later and your body may well succumb. In order to ensure that you stay healthy, despite your body's diminishing powers of self-protection, you should learn to become conscious even of minor symptoms. As soon as you notice an infection starting, for example, allow yourself to rest. Your

body will be far better able to survive if it can concentrate all its powers on defeating the threat.

You can use Bodypower to help you deal with specific symptoms and threats

Anxiety and depression

Anxiety and depression occasionally develop as a result of genuine difficulties. Commonly, however, they result from imagined failures. The man or woman who feel that he or she has let someone down, has failed someone or has failed to live up to his or her own expectations will suffer enormously as a result.

In these circumstances you may develop a vulnerability to irritations and stresses of varying kinds; problems which might otherwise have seemed relatively insignificant will often cause further emotional turmoil and the subsequent feelings of inadequacy will be self-reinforcing and self-perpetuating.

There are a number of things that you can do to strengthen your ability to resist the threats of imagined failure.

1 Recognise your own personality traits and where necessary make the changes which will strengthen your resistance.

2 Don't be afraid of making mistakes. Many people feel that if they have made a mistake they must

inevitably feel guilty. In fact,we learn only by making mistakes. The more successful a man is, the more mistakes he will have made.

3 Don't be afraid to change your mind. It takes strength not weakness to alter a decision or an opinion.

4 Learn to differentiate between the realistic expectations of those around you and the purely selfish expectations that they may harbour. Some of the people closest to you will be only too happy to take advantage of your kindness and goodwill. When you fail to satisfy their demands, they will make you feel guilty. And that can easily lead to anxiety and depression.

5 In Charles Dickens' Martin Chuzzlewit, Mark Tapley takes great pride in being cheerful in adversity. Tapley considers it a challenge to remain jolly in the midst of gloom. He repeatedly points out that anyone can be happy when things are going well, but that it takes strength of mind to remain cheerful when things are going badly. If you follow the Tapley philosophy you stand to gain a good deal. If you think about cheerful things, you'll work better and you'll feel better. There is even evidence that you will see and hear better when you're thinking pleasant thoughts!

6 Most of us use our imaginations against ourselves by always fearing the worst. Try to learn to use your imagination as a force for good. For example, if you are irritated by the telephone ringing and you find yourself rushing to answer it whatever you are doing,

you probably also find yourself worrying that it is going to bring bad news. If you ever do pluck up courage to let it ring and ring until it stops, you'll probably spend hours afterwards worrying about who was calling! And how urgent it was!

You suffer because your imagination tells you the worst. But you can change that. Sit down somewhere that you cannot hear the telephone if it should ring and relax your body and mind. Use the standard muscle and mind-relaxing techniques. When you've done this, imagine that you can hear a telephone ringing. And imagine that the person making the call has dialled a wrong number. Now imagine yourself sitting and letting the phone ring. Eventually the caller hangs up and cancels the call. Try this exercise a few times and you will slowly lose your fear of the telephone. You'll have recruited your imagination to work for you and not against you.

7 If you feel that you are inferior and you always see yourself failing, you will find that people will treat you as though you are inferior. And you will spend much of your life failing. Your body will eventually begin to prepare for failure as soon as you start anything. If, for example, you pick up a tray of crockery, you'll probably be able to see the shattered fragments! Your muscles will become tense and tight and your body will make adjustments that aren't needed in order to try and stop the accident you've foreseen. In all likelihood the tray will fall. Next time you carry a tray your imagination will be reinforced by your past unhappy experience. You'll go through life anxious and depressed.

Remember that neither the brain nor your body can tell real failure from imagined failure, nor real success from imagined success. If you look on the bright side, you'll acquire confidence and you'll be able to avoid anxiety and depression. There is, you see, a genuine physiological basis for positive thinking.

Waves of nausea

Motion sickness, or travel sickness , is one of those underestimated disorders. It's something that comedians often laugh at, but which sufferers find embarrassing as well as physically exhausting.

Since Hippocrates first described the problem a couple of thousand years ago many people have looked for ways to prevent and treat this most incapacitating disorder. Car sickness is one of the commonest types of motion sickness (perhaps only because more people travel by car than by any other type of vehicle) and dozens of possible solutions have been proposed. When I was a boy I used to suffer from car sickness and I remember my parents being inundated with advice from kindly relatives and friends. One aunt suggested that I eat a small mouthful of raw ginger before every journey. Another claimed that if I had a piece of stiff brown paper stuffed down the back of my shirt I would suffer no more. A third said if my father fixed a small length of chain to the back of the car I would have no more problems. None of these remedies worked.

More recently, researchers managed to produce some solid facts about motion sickness!

The first real progress was made by Army scientists, who were instructed to find ways in which soldiers being landed on enemy beaches could be protected against seasickness. The most important breakthroughs, however, were made by doctors involved in the American space programme.

Inspired by a need to find some way to protect astronauts from motion sickness, these researchers discovered that when the brain is receiving data about what is going on, it balances that flow of information against the motion and stops nausea developing. That's why car drivers, aeroplane pilots and bicycle riders don't usually suffer from motion sickness. It seems that sickness is far more likely to develop when the semi-circular canals which record movement are telling the brain that the body is in motion but the senses are providing no supporting information.

In other words, if you sit in a car and read a book your sense of balance will be providing information which is not backed up by sensory information.

To avoid motion sickness, therefore, you should ensure that you take an active interest in what is going on around you. If you're sitting in a car as a passenger you should look out for specific landmarks, road signs and so on.

By providing your brain with information, you'll be providing it with an explanation for the movement your body is recording. And you'll be less likely to suffer from motion sickness.

Eyes right

Orthodox medical practitioners are invariably sceptical. It seems almost a tradition that the profession should regard all new ideas as heretical and should dismiss original concepts as worthless or, at best, of dubious value.

When arguing in favour of their reactionary attitude, doctors will often explain that healing is a profession which attracts far more than its fair share of charlatans and quacks and that patients who are sick and desperate are easy game for individuals out to make a quick killing. However, you don't have to look very far when reading through a medical history book to see that a great many of the so-called charlatans have eventually been shown to have put forward sound, constructive ideas which have contributed much to the quality of practical medical care. It is wise, therefore, to keep an open mind about medical theories and to remember that Bacon, Galileo, Jenner and Darwin were all considered slightly odd by many of their colleagues.

One doctor who suffered rejection at the hands of the medical establishment was a New York eye specialist, Dr W. D. Bates. In the first years of this century, he did research and work on eye diseases which led him to the conclusion that defective vision is not due to permanent changes in the shape of the eye but to functional derangements.

Dr Bates argued that when the eye is used to look at an object, the external muscles which surround the eyeball are used to change the shape of the eye itself. He claimed that when a distant object is being examined, the external muscles move the back of the eye towards the lens, and that when a close object is being examined the opposite happens. He suggested that these muscular changes alter the shape of the eyeball and argued that individuals who are myopic (short sighted) or hypermetropic (long sighted) have eyeballs which have been misshapen by faulty action of the external muscles.

According to Bates, when a patient is myopic his eyeball is kept in a position which makes the viewing of distant objects difficult. On the other hand, when a patient suffers from hypermetropia the eyeball is kept in such a shape that the viewing of near objects is difficult.

Thus, if people with defective vision are really suffering because the external muscles of their eyeballs have been strained, the logical next step for the Bates theory was to suggest that they should learn to relieve the strain and tension on their eye muscles in order to improve their vision. When he put his theory in to practice Bates found that it worked. Not surprisingly, however, it was vehemently opposed by opticians, ophthalmologists and doctors.

Writing some years before the Austrian endocrinologist Hans Selye and his acolytes started to write about stress, Bates suggested that many people with strained eye muscles suffer from mental tension which has set up a corresponding physical strain on the eyes and, in particular, on the muscles which control them. Bates believed that tense, nervous people are more likely to develop defective vision than others and he stated that overwork, worry, fear and anxiety can all help damage the eyesight.

The Bates answer was to encourage his patients to learn how to relax themselves properly. He advocated both general exercises, designed to relax the whole body, and specific exercises, designed to relax the muscles around the eyeball. The following regime is based on the Bates philosophies and on Harry Benjamin's book Better Sight Without Glasses.

1 First you must learn how to relax your body and your mind. (See my previous advice on relaxation).

2 If you've ever stared at something very hard you'll know that the muscles of your eyes can get so tired that you eventually have to turn away and relax a little. Dr Bates had a technique called `palming', which he recommended to patients who wanted to know how to relax their eyes effectively. To do this you should sit in a very comfortable position, as loose and relaxed as you can get. Then close your eyes and cover them with your hands. Don't press on your eyes and leave your hands slightly cupped: there should be no direct pressure on your eyes at all.

Now you can either let the blackness gently fill your mind or, if you find it easier, allow images from your store of daydream scenes to fill your mind. Do this for ten minutes at a time, three times a day, if you have defective vision. Otherwise, do it whenever your eyes feel tired.

3 You should exercise the muscles of your neck and shoulders; if these are tight, they'll have a bad effect on the small muscles round your eyes. First raise your shoulders high. Then lower them. Do this a few times, after which you should try pushing your shoulders back as far as possible. When you've done that a few times, move your head as far forward as you can - try to touch your chest with your chin. Then move your head back so that your chin is as far away from your chest as possible. Finally, try turning your head to the right as far as it will go and then to the left as far as it will go. These are exercises that you should try if you get tension headaches or aching eyes.

4 You can also do some specific exercises to help relax the muscles round your eyes. Allow your eyes to go up into your head as far as possible. Keep your head still and don't strain the muscles at all - just take your eyes as far as they will go naturally. Next do a similar exercise taking your eyes as far left as they will go and then as far right as they will go. Again, keep your head as still as you can and don't strain your eyes. Finally, try holding up your index finger (either hand will do) a few inches in front of your eyes. Look at the finger and then look at any object in the distance. Look backwards and forwards between

your finger and the distant object ten times. Rest for a moment or two and then repeat the exercise. If you have defective vision you should practise these exercises several times a day.

5 You can use your imagination to improve your vision. Look at any line of print in this book. Concentrate hard on one word in the middle of the line and then close your eyes and imagine that you can see the one word far more clearly defined than the other words in the line. Open your eyes and look at the line again. Close your eyes and repeat the exercise. Keep doing this and when the whole word looks more clearly defined than the other words concentrate on smaller and smaller words - finally picking out individual letters for the exercise.

One of the reasons why Bates was so unpopular was undoubtedly the fact that he argued that by wearing spectacles people with bad eyes were merely making their sight worse and perpetuating their need for artificial aids. He pointed out that spectacles do nothing to help the existing problem, but are offered merely as an interventionist aid. They are intended to help the individual with a problem cope with that problem - not to help him overcome it. And there are several dangers.

The main danger, of course, is that by helping the patient who has defective vision to see with artificial aids the optician is ensuring that any muscle imbalance is maintained. The eyes are being prevented from recovering. Like those volunteers walking around with prism spectacles, whose eyes adapted, the individual wearing corrective spectacles will find that his eyesight adapts to fit his lenses. Spectacles can only aggravate and intensify a problem.

There isn't much chance of making a living out of teaching people how to cope with their visual problems by re-educating their muscles. And if all the people who wear spectacles were encouraged to give them up, many businesses would disappear overnight.

Nevertheless, there does seem to be evidence that some people who are prescribed spectacles can learn to manage without them. Naturally, people who already wear spectacles cannot simply give up their aids overnight. Their eyes will have grown accustomed to artificial support. What they can do is to try and give up their spectacles in easy stages - simply by not wearing them when they aren't doing anything demanding. Do the exercises I've described. Gradually, as the weeks go by, spectacles may have to be discarded and replaced with older, weaker lenses. That's a sign that progress is being made!

The dark enemy

Few disorders cause as much damage as cancer. The variety of illnesses which fall under this umbrella description cause many hundreds of thousands of deaths each year and produce much misery. And yet, despite the fact that few diseases have attracted so much attention from doctors and scientists, and despite the fact that much money and effort has been put into finding a cure for cancer, very little progress has been made.

We know that cancers usually develop when a group of cells within the body begin to divide and multiply too quickly and we know that this over-enthusiastic multiplication can be triggered by chemicals of various kinds. But we still do not know exactly how cancers develop and the orthodox remedies are often not only ineffective but so crude that they do as much damage to the host as to the cancer. Occasional, well-publicised breakthroughs have invariably promised much but delivered less.

What has become clear in recent years, however, is that there are simple, natural ways to treat cancer. Since they use the body's own healing powers, rather than drugs or pieces of expensive machinery, these techniques have been dismissed by orthodox practitioners as quack remedies and have been bracketed with such controversial therapies as apricot pit extract. Nevertheless, there is a growing amount of evidence to suggest that the best hope for the control of cancer may well come not from the laboratories of the world but from within the human body.

While traditional doctors round the world continue to concentrate exclusively on using remedies designed to attack the body and the cancers with knives, poisons, electricity and radiation, increasing numbers of practitioners are beginning to experiment with techniques designed to utilise some of the body's own defence mechanisms and to enhance the body's capacity for self-protection. These non-interventionist techniques are sometimes used as a genuine alternative to surgical and chemical remedies and sometimes as an adjunct. Either way the results are impressive.

A team with one of the greatest success rates in this very specialised area of treatment is that of Dr O. Carl Simonton and Stepanie Matthews-Simonton. Ms Matthews-Simonton is a psychotherapist and Carl Simonton is a medically qualified cancer specialist. Their work is described in Getting Well Again, which they wrote with James L. Creighton.

The basic principle upon which the Simontons have established their work is that negative emotions can contribute towards the development of cancer. It has been shown that something like three-quarters of all cancer patients become ill within a relatively short time of a major crisis in their lives. Psychologists claim that potential cancer patients often have difficulty in establishing close relationships, frequently tend to feel isolated and alone and may cover their internal feelings of inadequacy with an outward show of being comfortable, strong and stable.

The potential cancer patient is most at risk after some disruptive event. It seems that the pessimism and sense of doom invading the individual opens the way for the development of a life-threatening disorder.

The basis of the Simontons' work is that - just as negative emotions can contribute towards the development of cancer - so positive, cheerful emotions can help lead to a remission, if not a cure. They believe that by giving their cancer patients hope, a sense of cheerfulness and a feeling of pugnacious determination, they can help them fight apparently unstoppable disorders. Standard, interventionist anti-cancer techniques usually involve the use of weapons intended to help fight the cancer itself. There is not usually any room for the individual patient to play a part in his own recovery. And that, say the Simontons and those who do similar work, is wrong. Their success rate shows that the power of the body in the treatment of cancer can be immense. Used alongside traditional, interventionist techniques their approach produces dramatic effects.

Cancer sufferers can help themselves by enjoying themselves, by relaxing, by taking moderate exercise, by laughing, by having fun and by adding zest to their lives. They can also help themselves specifically by using their imagination to help overcome the threat posed by the cancer.

Here are some of the mental techniques that can be tried:

1 Imagine that the cancer cells are being thrown out of your body like rubbish that you're clearing out of your house. Imagine that the workmen are coming round every day to pick up fresh piles of unwanted cancer cells.

2 If you are being treated with drugs, imagine the drugs surging through your blood in search of cancer cells to destroy. Think of the drugs as your private cavalry.

3 Think of the white blood cells fighting off the cancer cells. Think of the white cells working alongside whatever drug you are taking.

4 Think of your cancer as being composed of individual, uncertain, homeless cells. The cancer is more frightened of you and your white cells than you are of it. Cancer doesn't always win and the cancer cells know that. Make sure you keep it on the defensive.

Happy birth day

One of the most controversial medical topics in recent years has been the question of whether pregnant women should have their babies in hospital or at home. The evidence is still inconclusive; for every survey showing that the risks to mother and baby are lower in hospital than at home, there is another equally reputable survey showing exactly the opposite.

Whatever the statistical truth may be, there is certainly powerful evidence to show that women who have their babies at home may well enjoy the experience more and may even have happier babies as a result.

Women who give birth in hospital are, I'm afraid, quite likely to find themselves given drugs they don't really need, artificially induced so that they will deliver at a convenient time and forced to adopt positions they find degrading and uncomfortable. And it is this last point which is perhaps the most significant of all, for a growing number of midwives and doctors agree that the position favoured by many obstetricians for childbirth is not comfortable, logical or physiologically sound. If a woman feels comfortable giving birth on all fours or on her side, she should be allowed to do so - such claims are now being made frequently.

One of the leading exponents of `natural childbirth' is Dr Michel Odent, who practices in Northern France and who argues that women should decide for themselves how they wish to give birth. He says that they should be allowed to respond to their own deepest instincts.

According to the Odent theory, if a woman wants to give birth to her baby while standing up. that is fine. If she wants to deliver her baby while squatting, then that is fine, too. Dr Odent even has women who deliver their babies while reclining under water.

Studies conducted in many countries confirm that in most cultures where women are allowed to choose their own position when giving birth, few choose to do so lying down. An impressive 82 per cent of women in 76 different cultures around the world give birth sitting, standing or squatting.

From these surveys it seems that when gravity is allowed to assist and the woman is allowed to choose a position that she finds comfortable, the need for pain-relieving drugs, instruments and other aids is greatly reduced.

It seems possible that those obstetricians who insist that they decide what positions their patients adopt may be perpetuating the need for drugs and artificial aids to help what is essentially an entirely natural process. Women who listen to their own bodies and who have their babies without interference invariably seem to go through childbirth with far less distress.

It is, incidentally, interesting to note that many of the midwives and doctors who favour natural childbirth on the grounds that it is better for the mother also claim that it is better for the baby too. They argue that the baby who enters a world full of harsh lights, stainless steel equipment, cold weighing scales and frightening noises will be subjected to a remarkable `culture' shock that can have lasting effects. And, if you stop to think about it, it may well be true that there is a shock to the system when a comfortable, warm, fluid-filled womb is suddenly exchanged for an artificial environment which most experienced adults themselves find slightly unnerving.

If you can't stand the heat

Your body is equipped with a number of magnificent temperature control mechanisms.

Theoretically, these are designed to ensure that your internal body temperature is kept at the right level notwithstanding the temperature outside. In practice, however, most of us refuse to allow our internal temperature control mechanisms to operate. When it is warm we switch on the air conditioning and when it is cold we add a couple of extra sweaters and turn up the central heating.

By replacing our inbuilt mechanisms this way we are damaging our ability to respond to temperature changes. Those marvellous inner mechanisms are being encouraged to atrophy because we are consciously taking over the work they are supposed to do. By denying our in built mechanisms the chance to work and by becoming more and more reliant on artificial aids, we are steadily making ourselves more and more vulnerable to changes in our environmental conditions. Because we are accustomed to air conditioning and central heating we suffer more than we need when we are caught unexpectedly in an unheated railway carriage or when we have to make our way between two fully heated buildings.

Now, I recognise that no one is going to want to switch off the central heating or the air conditioning altogether. But if you want to make sure that your body's temperature control mechanisms aren't destroyed and that you can still respond to temperature changes, I suggest that you follow the notes I've compiled:

1 Try not to alter the temperature within your building too much from the temperature outside. If the temperature difference is too great, your body's control mechanism will not be able to cope.

2 When the weather outside is very cold and you are working or living in a heated building put on plenty of clothes before you go outside to ensure that the shock to your body is kept to a minimum. Your temperature control mechanisms are designed to cope with gradual changes in the environmental temperature, rather than sudden swings from boiling hot to freezing cold. When the manufacturer prepared the specifications for your body he wasn't aware that you were going to be able to move from arctic conditions to equatorial conditions in five seconds.

3 There is probably some truth in the old-fashioned theory that you shouldn't go outside in to the cold immediately after taking a hot bath or shower. When you're in a hot bath your superficial circulatory system will be well dilated to help you lose body heat. If you go outside with your blood vessels in that condition your body temperature may fall dangerously low - and your temperature control mechanisms may not be able to cope.

4 Finally, if your body's temperature control mechanisms seem to have atrophied and you find it difficult to deal with temperature changes, take heart; for there are ways in which you can exercise your body's ability to respond to the temperature of the environment. There are, indeed, ways in which you can force your body to respond appropriately!

A few years ago, Christina Maslach of the Department of Psychology at the University of California, Berkeley, and Garry Marshall and Phillip G. Zimbardo of the Department of Psychology at Stanford University, showed that individuals can control their own body temperature voluntarily. Inspired, perhaps, by the work of the Russian Professor Luria (whom we met earlier in this book), who described how a subject he observed could make one hand get hotter by imagining that it was resting on a hot stove while at the same time he made the other colder by imagining that it was holding a piece of ice, these researchers provided some amazing results, succeeding in demonstrating that it is perfectly possible to change skin temperature voluntarily.

That original research has now been taken one step further. In the Journal of the American Medical Association recently a report from the American National Institute of Health suggested that patients who suffer from a disorder called Raynaud's Phenomenon may be able to benefit from this type of technique.

Patients who suffer from Raynaud's Phenomenon get painfully cold hands when the external temperature falls because for some reason the arteries supplying their fingers overreact. The vessels become very tightly constricted and the supply of blood to the fingers is reduced to a mere trickle. Normally, patients with this disorder are encouraged to keep their bodies warm - by keeping the internal body temperature as high as possible it is not too difficult to limit the extent to which the arteries shut down.

However, the report that was published in JAMA suggests that patients with this disease can control their body temperature themselves and can therefore control the rate at which their arteries constrict. The patients in the study were taught to relax and to imagine that they were lying on a beach underneath the warm sun. Their imaginary sunshine proved strong enough to convince their bodies that they were warm even when they were cold.

If you are not a sufferer from Raynaud's Phenomenon you may none the less like to try this simple trick next time you feel particularly cold and can't get near a fire. Conversely, if you're suffering from too much heat you might like to try imagining that you're on an ice floe somewhere!

A vein thought

Blood that has deposited its oxygen and food to the tissues travels back to the heart and lungs through the veins. These thin-walled vessels are filled with valves and blood moves inside them only when the muscles through which they travel constrict. The tightening muscles squeeze the veins, and push the blood along. The valves stop the blood flowing back again.

If for some reason the blood doesn't move along the veins fast enough the veins may become gorged with fluid. Swollen veins, which are often sore, are usually described as `varicose'. the veins in the legs are most commonly affected because there the blood has to fight its way upwards against the pull of gravity.

Varicose veins are particularly common among people who have to spend a lot of their time standing relatively still. Dentists and shop assistants, for example, regularly suffer. Their blood is allowed to collect in the veins because there isn't enough muscle movement to keep it moving upwards.

If you are at high risk, you may be able to help yourself by deliberately contracting the muscles in your calves every few minutes. Do this and the muscle movement will keep the blood travelling upwards even when you seem to be standing still.

The human body is not designed for standing. It's designed for moving. Varicose veins only develop when a natural *Bodypower* isn't given a proper chance to work.

Indigestion

Indigestion, wind, dyspepsia, peptic ulcers, gastritis, nausea and heartburn are all common problems. Millions of people are regularly afflicted by these uncomfortable symptoms, any of which can be a sign that the body is protesting. Although stress is frequently a basic cause of stomach problems, the specific symptoms can often be induced by eating the wrong things at the wrong time. If you try to identify exactly how you feel, then you may be able to come to a conclusion about the cause - and produce some answers that will help.

For example, if you find yourself feeling uncomfortably full and if you suffer from a bloated feeling when you've eaten, your problem may have been caused by eating too much or eating too quickly. When you push large quantities of food in to your stomach very rapidly you run the risk of overloading the system within. Your stomach is not huge and it can only produce a limited amount of gastric juice to help digest the food it receives. If you overload it, you'll distend its walls and acquire an unpleasant feeling inside.

If you deliberately try to taste the food you eat, you'll probably find yourself automatically limiting the rate at which you swallow food. Put down your knife and fork between mouthfuls if you can't manage to slow yourself down any other way.

If you feel as though there is a lump of undigested food in your stomach, that may in fact be the case. And it may be that you're not chewing properly. Food has to be well chewed if it is going to be properly digested, for the saliva that is produced in your mouth contains special enzymes which help to prepare the food for the secretions it will meet in your stomach. The answer is obvious - spend a little more time chewing!

Finally, do try to be aware of any specific foodstuffs that upset your stomach. If you experience nausea every time you eat fatty foods, you should avoid them. If cucumber `doesn't like you', keep off the cucumber. If you get dyspepsia or wind every time you eat sprouts, avoid sprouts. Your stomach isn't a dustbin and although the acid it contains is powerful there are still some foods which can upset it. If your symptoms disappear entirely when you have avoided one particular food, you can try reintroducing that item a few weeks later. If the symptoms reappear, you will probably be wise to keep off that type of food indefinitely. Although not all sufferers will obtain complete relief from this simple approach, most will obtain some.

Moving experiences

Many people treat their bowels like unruly pets or naughty children - punishing them with powerful drugs when they don't behave properly. Men and women who suffer from constipation regularly use laxatives in order to establish an acceptable pattern of bowel behaviour.

The use of laxative drugs is illogical because many bowel disorders, and in particular constipation, are caused because the wrong sort of foods have been eaten. Using a drug to deal with a problem caused by bad eating habits is about as logical as using buckets to collect water entering through places where there should be roof tiles. They are both suitable short-term solutions, but there are much better ways to deal with the underlying causes.

Bowel disorders develop commonly these days because our diet often consists largely of highly refined foods. Our bowels haven't evolved to deal with these new types of food. The muscles of the bowel wall like to have something to squeeze and the quantity and quality of waste material passing through the bowels plays an important and very basic part in a number of fundamental physiological processes.

If you want to avoid bowel problems you should eat a roughage-rich diet. Give your intestines the sort of food they were designed to cope with and they will work far more efficiently.

A joint approach

In the last few decades millions of pounds have been spent on the search for a cure for arthritis. Hundreds of drug companies and thousands of researchers have struggled to find an explanation for a disease that has crippled millions of sufferers. And despite the fact that very many `breakthroughs' have been made and journals have published articles describing wonderful new theories, none of the scientists working on the subject has yet managed to come up with any real answers. They have, of course, produced many new drugs. All these have some use as painkillers and anti-inflammatory aids, but none of them helps to prevent symptoms developing or makes them disappear permanently once they have arrived.

One of the best explanations for the way that arthritis affects the human body has come from a doctor who wasn't funded by a rich organisation and who hasn't received praise from other members of his own profession. His account of the way that arthritis affects the human body is nevertheless logical.

Dr William W. Fox is a London practitioner who has specialised in the treatment of patients with various forms of arthritis for many years. He believes that both rheumatoid and osteoarthritis develop in the same way and that both are caused by the body's reaction to a virus. In Arthritis: Is your suffering really necessary?, he explains that if the disease develops quickly the patient will acquire symptoms of rheumatoid arthritis, whereas if its onset is slow the patient will acquire the symptoms of osteoarthritis. In both cases, the arthritis is a consequence of the body reacting to an infection.

Most important of all is Dr Fox's claim that he can recognise the existence of this most damaging of diseases in the very early stages, before obvious signs develop. Consequently, he is able to help people stop arthritis developing. He claims that in the early phases the patient will complain of aches and pains in his joints and of a general feeling of being unwell. These vague symptoms are, he suggests, too often ignored. He adds that when they are ignored, trouble begins. His most important suggestion is that anyone who notices a generalised ache or a localised pain should listen to what is effectively a warning sign - and rest!

Although Dr Fox doesn't mention any of the other principles of *Bodypower* in his book, what he is describing is, in fact, nothing more than a specific variation on the theme I've used as the basis for *Bodypower*. Dr Fox thinks that arthritis develops when we ignore the signs telling us that our bodies are affected by a potentially damaging virus. And he suggests that if we only listen and rest when we have other odd aches and pains that we cannot explain, we won't develop arthritis. Dr Fox believes that rest is not only the best answer to the virus, and the best way to prevent symptoms developing, but that it is also the best way to help reduce the pain and stiffness of an acute attack.

Migraine

Migraine headaches can be cruelly incapacitating. Sufferers have to put up with headaches, nausea, mood changes, sensitivity to noise and light, itchy eyes, stuffed-up noses and a host of other annoying symptoms. The headaches can be particularly severe and very difficult to treat.

Although there are still some mysteries about precisely what happens during a migraine attack, it seems that the problems are largely a result of the body's response to stress. Misled into thinking that it can cope with the stress by preparing the muscles for immediate action, the body increases the blood supply to the muscles and closes down the supply to the brain. Then, when the threat seems to be lifting, the vessels open up again and the blood surges back through. It is this renewed flow of blood which seems to cause the pain of a migraine attack.

Many sufferers find that they can ease the severity of their attacks. Methods include avoiding stress; learning to cope with pressures more effectively; limiting exposure to specific foods or types of problems which make symptoms worse; and using drugs which interfere with the constriction of the blood vessels.

But these techniques are often far from satisfactory and so it's very good news for migraine sufferers that it is sometimes possible to use *Bodypower* to overcome a response that has been triggered in turn by an inappropriate *Bodypower* response.

Since the symptoms of migraine are caused by a constriction of the blood vessels supplying the brain, it is clear that any effective *Bodypower* treatment must help reverse that process. If you're going to stop the migraine developing, you've got to stop the blood vessels constricting.

Until fairly recently no one could see how it could be possible to do this. After all, you can't see or feel the arteries supplying your brain and so how can you possibly tell whether your efforts are working?

And then someone noticed that migraine sufferers often have cold hands and cold feet and someone else pointed out that when the vessels to the brain are constricted by the body's response to stress the vessels to the skin and to the hands and feet are also constricted.

And that provided the clue!

For although it isn't possible to tell whether or not you are succeeding in opening up, and keeping open, the arteries which supply your brain, it is possible to tell whether or not your attempts to open up the vessels supplying your hands are successful. The *Bodypower* answer to migraine consists, therefore, of conscious attempts to divert blood into the peripheral system which supplies your hands. If you can do this, and get your hands warmer, then you'll also be diverting blood into the vessels supplying your brain - and thereby avoiding a migraine.

If you are a migraine sufferer who has been under a lot of pressure, or if you've just had an aura suggesting that a migraine attack might be coming try this technique:

1 Relax yourself physically and mentally. Use the techniques already described.

2 Try to see the blood vessels which supply your hands and try to see them getting wider and wider. See more and more blood flowing into the tissues. If you find that difficult, try to imagine that you've got your hands held up in front of a fire. Or imagine that you're lying on a warm beach.

3 You should slowly become aware of your hands getting warmer and warmer. As this happens the

blood supply to your brain will also be increased and your migraine attack will be aborted.

Pain control

Frightening and uncomfortable as it may be, pain is nevertheless a vital protective mechanism. The presence or absence of pain provides our brain with vital information and acts as an essential, automatic feedback device. Although there is much that we don't understand about how it develops, we know that pain can be affected dramatically by the psychological state of the individual concerned. Someone who is under tremendous pressure or stress will be unlikely to notice physical pain. An individual who is under a moderate amount of pressure may, on the other hand, suffer far more than an individual who is under no stress. Negative feelings, such as fear and anxiety, can enhance pain. And positive feelings, such as joy and happiness, can greatly reduce the amount of perceived pain.

From the bewildering array of (often confusing) facts that are available about pain, we know that much can be done to minimise the effect it has, to bring it under control. I've collected together some signposts to pain control.

1 Remember that pain is a device used by your body to tell you that something is wrong. If you are in pain the first thing you should do is look for a cause. And then search for a way to deal with the cause. Pain is

a symptom of an underlying problem and the only long-term solution is to treat the cause.

2 In a crisis your body will be able to overcome the limitations imposed by pain. If you're injured while fighting for your life, you'll probably remain almost unaware of the extent of your injuries. If you're playing in an important sporting fixture, you'll probably be able to disregard pain which might have been totally incapacitating in a less important contest. It is the body's own painkilling hormones which enable you to ignore pain in this way. Useful as these hormones are, however, it is vital to remember that the pain you are ignoring was originally intended to help protect the injured part of your body. If you injure your leg, for example, and then continue to use it, you are bound to run the risk of exacerbating the injury.

3 Painkilling sprays and injections are popular among sportsmen. It is important to remember that these aids deaden a symptom which was originally designed for your protection. By deadening the pain and enabling you to continue as if there had been no injury at all, they make you run a real risk of permanently damaging the tissues that the pain was intended to protect.

4 If you are feeling tense, you will be more susceptible to pain than if you are calm and comfortable. When you are under stress your whole body will be prepared for emergency action. A small threat will be likely to produce an unexpectedly large response - and an unjustified amount of pain. To

reduce your pain threshold, learn how to relax your body and your mind.

5 Fear magnifies pain. If you find a strange lump somewhere on your body and you are worried about it, you will suddenly find yourself extraordinarily aware of everything going on in your body. Every minor ache, every tiny twinge will be magnified. For most of us our greatest fear is of the unknown. If your imagination is allowed to rule, you will fear the worst and suffer accordingly. It follows, therefore, that if you are worried about your health you should seek advice, identify and face your fears.

6 Pain is something that we all use to our advantage from time to time. As children we learn that if we are in pain we will receive sympathy and attention, kindness and love. The rewards of pain can often be great. You must understand this, because if you are obtaining great rewards from your pain, your body will see to it that the pain continues.

7 Very few pains are consistently bad. Most pains come and go. If you can find out when your pain is getting worse, you should also be able to decide why it is getting worse. There are sometimes simple, straightforward explanations. For example, if your pain is only bad in the evenings, there is a chance that for some reason the amount of stress you endure goes up in the evenings. Perhaps you find it difficult to get on with some evening caller? Or perhaps you have special responsibilities at that time of day which you find daunting?

8 A number of experts have developed specific ways in which you can use your body's resources to help you cope with pain. Among those prominent in this field are Dr C. Norman Shealy of the Pain and Health Rehabilitation Center in La Crosse, Wisconsin, Dr David Bresler of the Pain Clinic at the UCLA School of Medicine and Dr O. Carl Simonton of the Cancer Counselling and Research Center in Fort Worth, Texas. Four pain control techniques are described below; but before you try them you must relax your body and your mind as described earlier.

a. To ensure that you get the best out of your body you should try to visualise your own healing resources at work. Try to see white cells in your blood heading towards the site of your pain and taking with them valuable pain-relieving endorphins. If the white cells find any infection, cancer or damaged tissue, envisage them reorganising the tissues,tearing away damaged material and repairing what can be salvaged. If there is no obvious damage there, try to see the white cells encouraging the muscle fibres to relax. As all this happens, you'll slowly notice the pain disappearing.

b. Try to think of the pain as an invader of some sort that has managed to find its way into your body. See it as clearly as you can. Then try to ask the invader why it is there. You may find this difficult to begin with, but if you persevere you should be able to establish some sort of dialogue. What you are doing, of course, is analysing your responses to the world around you.

The invader may surprise you with its answers. You may find that you are in pain because you are worried about something, because you are feeling miserable about something, because you have got to do something that is worrying you - or for some other unexpected reason. Once you have isolated the reason for the presence of the pain you can try to decide precisely what you need to do to make it disappear. Continue your conversation by asking the invader under what circumstances it would be prepared to leave you alone. You may find that there is some specific piece of advice that you can follow.

c. Try taking yourself outside your own body and looking at your body as though it belonged to a stranger. Now try soothing that stranger's body and try offering comfort and support. Stroke his brow gently. Gradually you'll see the pain begin to disappear. When the body is pain-free you can re-enter it.

d. Imagine that the sensation of pain is being transmitted round your body with the aid of telephone wires. Now make yourself a pair of imaginary wire cutters and systematically take them round your body cutting each of the wires in turn.

9 Many people who are in pain seem to deny themselves pleasure and those around them often fail to offer fun as a remedy. It sometimes seems that to talk about pain and pleasure in the same breath would be wrong. But sadness makes pain worse - why shouldn't happiness make it easier?

10 When a small boy falls and cuts himself, his mother will often kiss him and his wound. The phrase `kiss it better' is a part of the English language. It isn't the kiss that does the job, of course, but the affection and love behind it. Anyone in pain will benefit from either or both.

11 If you've ever had a bad bump and have tried rubbing the spot to help clear away the pain you'll know that this unorthodox form of treatment often seems to work. Until fairly recently this mechanism was something of a mystery, but it seems that rubbing, pressing and stroking a painful spot all help eradicate pain, both by inhibiting the passage of nerve impulses and by triggering the production of pain-relieving hormones. There is also evidence that vibrators will help relieve pain in much the same sort of way.

I do not, of course, promise that these various pain-relieving techniques will work all the time or that they will always make pain disappear entirely. But such natural techniques will help you cope with pain. You need to practise them, because as your body needs practice if it is to acquire a sporting skill, so it needs practice if you are to acquire a pain-control skill. If you do practice, however, these techniques will enable you to use *Bodypower* to help control your pains.

You can use Bodypower to help improve your life style

Breaking bad habits

Bad habits, such as stuttering, nail-biting and smoking, are nothing more than simple physical signs that you are reaching your stress threshold. You may be able to help yourself cope with these unwelcome traits by reducing your exposure to stress, but if it is imagined pressure which is causing your problems the attempt is likely to produce stresses of its own.

You'll be more successful if you enlist the help of your imagination, especially because it was probably your imagination which helped push you past your stress threshold in the first place.

As always, the principle of *Bodypower* is to use your body's strengths rather than to fight against them.

To give up nail-biting, for example, follow this simple regime:

1 Think of the sort of situation in which you are most likely to bite your nails. You may, for instance, find yourself most under pressure when meeting strangers.

2 Think back and remember everything you felt on a specific occasion when you felt the need to bite your nails. Re-create the fears, anxieties and apprehensions which went through your mind. Try to

`feel' the atmosphere again. Try to `see' your surroundings.

3 And now see yourself coping perfectly well. Your nails have grown and you look smart and presentable. Keep up the fantasy, wave your hands about.

4 Repeat this exercise several times a day. Every day. See yourself in a variety of stressful situations. And see yourself conquering the problem without biting your nails. The power of the imagination is great. You will slowly replace a bad memory with a good memory. and nail-biting will eventually become a thing of the past.

Do not be discouraged if your new pattern of behaviour doesn't take over immediately. If you still find yourself biting your nails when under pressure, keep practising the regime I've outlined. Bad habits don't suddenly appear overnight and they don't usually disappear in a few hours either.

Enhanced serendipity

Have you noticed how the solutions to difficulties tend to come when you least expect them? After struggling unsuccessfully to find the answer to a specific problem you'll probably find that the solution unexpectedly pops into your mind when you're walking down the garden, watching television, or like Archimedes, lying in the bath.

And have you noticed how often you get hunches, flashes of inspiration and your best and brightest ideas when you're on holiday or relaxing and doing nothing in particular?

Many of the world's greatest thinkers have described their moments of glory and have provided the background evidence for the theory that the brain is often much better able to sort out problems when it is left to think things through by itself. Feed in all the necessary and available information and your brain will continue to sift through all the possibilities while you get on with something else.

Don't be afraid to take advantage of this unusual human facility. You can't deliberately use your brain's automatic capabilities but you can enhance the chances of your benefitting from them by learning how to relax properly. Pile in the information, throw in a few possible solutions and wait and see what happens!

Sense and sensibility

Under normal circumstances the brain is continually being flooded with messages from all the sensory organs. Only if one message is unusually powerful will it break through and produce a response. That's why blind people so often have such exceptionally acute hearing. Because their brains don't receive any visual impulses, there is far more chance of auditory impulses getting a good hearing.

You can improve your susceptibility to particular types of sensory message by reducing the input from other sensory organs. If you're listening to something and you want to get the best out of your ears, you'll do so if you close your eyes. Similarly, if you're looking at something and you want to use your eyes to best advantage you can try cutting out all auditory impulses. If you want to get the best out of your taste buds, you should close your eyes in a quiet room.

The sporting life

If you are a keen follower of any sport, you will undoubtedly have heard your favourite stars admitting that one of the most important secrets for success is to have the right mental approach. However good a golfer may be on the practice grounds he won't win any big tournaments if he can't relax properly when he's playing. Those $20,000 putts will never go in for the golfer who is tense, anxious and desperate to win. The same is true for all sports stars. The urge to win must be there, of course, but the tennis player who suffers too much from nerves will never walk away with the big trophy. The racing driver who gets the jitters before a race may well have the fastest practice lap, but when it matters he'll either be left behind or he'll be sitting in a heap of crumpled metal.

In this respect you and I are not different. Having the correct approach is just as important for the learner as it is for anyone else. If you allow stress and tension to interfere with your skills, you will never be able to play as well as you could play. On the other hand if you use your *Bodypower* to the full when you're playing your favourite sport, you'll be able to do yourself justice every time. *Bodypower* cannot turn a 24 handicap golfer into a successful tournament pro, but it can ensure that he (or she) plays as well as he is physically capable.

To become more successful at your chosen sport you have to acquire an automatic system which can take over for you. Use the following notes:

1 Once in every game most players will play one shot of which they are really proud. A golfer will flight an iron shot onto the green. A tennis player will serve an ace. Every time you do this it is important to remember the feel of the shot. Remember how your body felt and keep a clear picture of your surroundings. Recall the weather, the temperature, what you were wearing... and so on. If you can play that shot once, you can play it again. But to do so you have to be certain that your body remembers how you played the shot the first time.

2 Practice done under no pressure at all is invaluable. If you're going to acquire a sporting skill you must develop a number of muscle memories and reflex actions. You must develop certain muscle rhythms so that when you're playing under pressure you can play by memory. Every time you play a particular shot when you're practising, remember how you felt - that is, if it's a good shot! When you play a bad shot, ignore it - forget it ever happened.

3 Next time you're playing an important match and you want to do your best, try to switch onto automatic pilot as much as you can. Top international tennis players (and for that matter top international concert pianists) don't think before they move their fingers and hands. They act according to carefully developed reflexes. You must do the same, and allow your imagination, memory and *Bodypower* to play the shots for you.

4 Remember those super shots you've played in the past? The ones that you were proud of and that you stored up in memories? Those are the ones that can help you play your best. Each time you're about to play a shot try to recall the last time you played such a shot well. Feel the wind and the sun and imagine how you felt and what happened. The bigger the library of your memories the easier it will be. Your imagination has to convince your body that it is taking over again and it has to set your muscles in exactly the right way....When your play your memory shot your imagination and your muscles will themselves take over, thereby removing the risk of your fears, pessimism and anxieties interfering with your abilities. Before you play your shot, remember what happened last time - when you played your winner! And leave your body to do the rest.

Smile and the world smiles with you

You can use other people's *Bodypower* facilities to help you with your personal relationships.

For example, if you smile at someone every time he uses a certain word you will soon discover that he will unconsciously use that particular word more and more often. He'll be getting an appreciative response from you and he'll respond accordingly. He won't know he's doing it but - however much we like to think of ourselves as aggressive - most of us are very anxious to please those around us. Our *Bodypower* principles tell us that it is good if others like us. And so that man or woman you're smiling at will unconsciously know that he is pleasing you.

Similarly, if you smile at someone every time he does something you want him to keep on doing, you'll find that he'll repeat the action. He may not know that he is repeating it and he certainly won't know why. But he'll be happy and so will you.

Mothers, lovers and salesmen round the world have for years relied on this automatic response. They probably never knew what they were doing or why. But you do - and you can benefit, too!

And finally...

The end of the line

In some parts of the world voodoo is no joke. It is a deadly serious matter. If an individual is told that he is going to die, he will die. If he is told that he is going to develop a paralysis, he will develop a paralysis. The power of the man operating the voodoo curse is absolute and he can literally kill with a word or two.

Most of us in the Western world find all this mildly amusing. We feel comfortably able to ignore such threats in the knowledge that they could never be used on us. We'd never take any notice of them, we tell ourselves. And yet in our own way we are just as vulnerable to the curse and to magic as any individual suffering under the power of a malevolent witch doctor. The difference is merely this: instead of listening to and believing curses pronounced by men wearing wild costumes we tend to listen and believe prognoses announced by men wearing white coats.

If a doctor in a white coat tells a man that he is going to die, that man will probably die. The suggestion is not an extreme one - the evidence bears it out. People who have been told wrongly that they have cancer will suddenly fade away and die. I myself know someone who was told that he had lung cancer, following which he lost weight, looked deathly and began to fade fast, Assured later that a mistake had been made and that he had a treatable infection, he quickly put the weight back on and made a marvellous recovery.

The simple truth is that whether the information comes from a man dressed in feathers with a string of beads round his neck or from a man in a white coat with a stethoscope round his neck, it is faith that does the damage. If the individual on the receiving end of the spell or bad news believes what he is told, his imagination will do the rest. Indeed, some patients can sink into a steady decline through their own attitude, without input from anyone else. They can convince themselves that they are going to die. And then they will turn their heads to the wall and prepare themselves for death. Occasionally, the curse may even come from someone bringing good news. For example, I remember a staunchly religious patient who was seriously ill, but not dying, and who was visited by a priest. The patient thought that the priest had arrived to give him the last rites and he died within minutes. The patient had responded to his own faith and his own imagination and condemned himself.

All this is frightening and disturbing, but there is, of course, another way of looking at the power of the imagination. For just as patients have died because they have had no faith that they will live, so patients have survived and bloomed because they have refused to accept the bad news that they have been given. Just as fear and anxiety can kill, so hope, determination and delight can delay death. By harnessing *Bodypower*, individuals who have been told that they are soon to die have succeeded in cheating death. We have powers of which too few of us are aware. We should use them.

For details of other books by Vernon Coleman please see his Amazon Author page or visit http://www.vernoncoleman.com/

If you found this book useful we would be grateful if you would post a review on Amazon. Thank you.

Made in the USA
Las Vegas, NV
23 March 2021

19971064R00120